12¹/₂ STEPS TO SPIRITUAL HEALTH

"Our promise is freedom in Christ. *12½ Steps to Spiritual Health* is a **valuable tool** to help us make this promise a reality. When faithfully worked through, within the context of supportive relationships, it will enable us to move out of our brokenness to a place of greater security in Christ. It is an ideal resource for any member of a cell group."
– *Liz West, Director of Cell UK, Leader of St Albans Chapel Fellowship*

"We are all addicts and need help in order to move on in our journey with God. **This book is encouraging** and the steps are attainable. With liberal applications of God's grace and the knowledge that he doesn't show us all our sin at once (or we would sink without trace) it will help many of us not to give up, but keep going."
– *Christine Noble, Pioneer*

"The challenge is to mobilize the body of Christ to include every member in ministry. To see that happen we must help people to help themselves in God's power to be whole. **This book makes a major contribution** to this process. Its step-by-step approach will help many to be whole and mobilized."
– *Laurence Singlehurst, Director, YWAM England*

12½
Steps to
Spiritual
Health

Howard Astin

MONARCH
BOOKS

Mill Hill, London & Grand Rapids, Michigan

First published by Monarch Books in the UK in 2002,
Concorde House, Grenville Place, Mill Hill, London NW7 3SA.

Distributed by:
UK: STL, PO Box 300, Kingstown Broadway,
Carlisle, Cumbria CA3 0QS;
USA: Kregel Publications, PO Box 2607,
Grand Rapids, Michigan 49501.

ISBN 1 85424 579 1

British Library Cataloguing Data
A catalogue record for this book is available
from the British Library.

Designed and produced for the publisher by
Gazelle Creative Productions,
Concorde House, Grenville Place, Mill Hill,
London NW7 3SA.

Acknowledgements

Thanks to my wife and children for their support and encouragement, even though I had promised not to write a second book!

Also, thanks again to all the members of St John's, Bowling, for their continued inspiration to me and their willingness to go $12^{1}/_{2}$ stepping.

Contents

Introduction

The 12$^{1}/_{2}$ Step Programme

This book is about steps that need to be taken in order for church members to be mobilized and to be free to serve. In my previous book, *Body & Cell*[1], I set out the challenge that had been given to us at St John's, Bowling, Bradford to change our church structures in order for the members to be mobilized. The challenge went to the core of what we were as a church. It questioned our vision and also the values that we held dear. This in turn led us to examine just how free we were to carry out God's commission. We developed teaching and training to facilitate this process of change.

This teaching and training now takes the form of 12$^{1}/_{2}$ Steps. It has been developed from the "12 Step Programme" pioneered by Alcoholics Anonymous and various other self-help "Anonymous" groups. These Anonymous groups have been a source of healing and help to many who are addicted in one way or another (e.g. to alcohol, drugs or gambling). However, what we have found is that the core of the teaching through the 12 Step Programme is first of all biblical and secondly powerful for all Christians, not just for those who have some recognized addiction. In the course of developing this programme, we found it necessary to include an additional step – Step 4$^{1}/_{2}$.

The realization that this programme was to be powerful in freeing and mobilizing our membership came slowly to me and the leadership at St John's. I had been aware of the 12 Step Programme ever since I arrived at St John's in 1988. Already there were about 20 or so adult members within the congregation who had actually found faith in Jesus through the 12 Step Programme of Alcoholics Anonymous. They had then started coming to St John's but still spoke about how they lived out the programme within their lives. Indeed, they talked of how the programme enabled them to live out the teachings of the Bible in a practical way. Over the years and through many conversations and experiences I have come to see that this 12 Step Programme has much to offer *all* Christians. It can be quite dynamic, by setting people free from all manner of encumbrances that bind them in the present and stop them becoming fully mobilized in the work of the kingdom.

The 12 Steps are well known in the United States, but in the UK they are relatively unknown. Here they have been adapted slightly to go back to their true Christians roots and to the way they were originally intended to be used. The main difference is that the full Alcoholics Anonymous 12 Steps would talk of "God as you understand him", whereas the founders of the movement, Dr Bob and Bill W, a drunkard doctor and a stockbroker, always acknowledged Jesus to be the revelation of God the Father here on earth. More recently, Christians have taken up the 12 Steps and used them in church ministry, particularly to help people with addictions. Movements such as "Overcomers" use these principles to challenge existing church members who see they have problems that may be based in addictions. At St John's we have now applied the 12 Steps to all our members. New Christians take the 12 Steps as part of our nurture course, and all existing members have been challenged to work through the 12 Steps. This means we have an effective tool to kickstart the journey to become more and more like Jesus.

Part of our vision and values

It has been very exciting to see how the 12 Step Programme has helped us fulfil our vision statement as a cell church and to work out in practice the values we hold. We have a simple vision statement, which says we are "to know God, to show God, to share God". Although this vision statement was adopted before we began using the 12 Step Programme, it was so encouraging to find that the last Step, which sums up what the previous Steps have been about, actually reflected the content of our vision statement. It talks of us having a spiritual encounter (to know God), to practice the principles learnt (to show God), and to convey the message to others (to share God).

The values of our church are:

1. Jesus at the centre
2. Positive faith in God
3. Every-member ministry
4. Caring community
5. Living for the lost

We began to see how these values were reflected in the 12 Steps and complemented our Arrival Kit. They focus on the Lordship of Jesus for the individual and for the congregation, reflecting the value of *Jesus at the centre*.

Then we saw how many of our members were afflicted by doubt and disappointment or by negative rather than positive attitudes. This is tackled by the Steps and is a useful tool in bringing people back to *positive faith in God*.

Some members found that things of the past, situations in the present or attitudes towards the future stopped them being effective ministers for the Lord. The Steps helped to free them so that they were mobilized and ready to serve, thereby reflecting our value *every-member ministry*.

God has called us to be a *caring community* at St John's and over the years has taught us much about how to do this within our cell groups. The Steps have given added impetus to putting this value into practice. Members of cells have cared for each other and gone to a deeper level of commitment and love for one another, by praying and seeking healing for one another. When we come to Steps 4, 4^1/$_2$ and 5, the extent to which this depth of relationship can grow will be evident.

There is no greater motivation for reaching out to people who do not know the Lord than a deep thankfulness for what he has done for us. For years we have known that the commitment of our leadership often depends upon the depth of thankfulness that the leader has towards the Lord. This thankfulness enables him or her to keep going when things get tough. So when people experience the transforming power of God as a result of taking these 12 Steps, then they want to pass on the message of how others in need can be likewise helped. So we see our members take up the challenge to start *living for the lost*.

The Steps are biblical and beneficial

Before taking you through the Steps in detail, let me emphasize that they are not additional to the teaching of the Bible. Each Step has a biblical foundation, and in a methodical way reveals our human condition and shows the path to true spiritual healing and freedom. That these Steps should come from people whom society would denigrate seems to be in keeping with biblical teaching. Take 1 Corinthians 1:27, for example: "But God chose the foolish things of the world to shame the wise; God chose the weak things of the world to shame the strong."

In recent years I have had many opportunities to speak to groups of ministers and I was initially surprised to find how many were hungry for some tool to enable healing in church members. Obviously there are people in every congregation who have evident problems and afflictions, but many ministers have recognized that God is calling them to go to a much deeper awareness of the encumbrances that afflict so many. For example, there has been a growth in "encounter weekends" which encourage church members to look at some of the real issues of their lives such as habitual sins, hurts and guilt. These things so often hinder their sanctification and restrict the effectiveness of their witness.

Although many of these encounter weekends are powerful and effective, there is in my opinion no substitute for having such teaching as part of the on-going nurture course within a church. The 12 Step Programme has the added advantage of being spread over some period of time, as time is necessary for healing and change to be effected within the individual. Initially when we preached on the Steps at St John's, we found it necessary to have a two-month gap between Steps 7 and 8. People needed this space to fully work through some of the fundamental Steps – 4, $4^{1}/2$ and 5 in particular.

The 12 Steps do go uncomfortably deep. But they cleanse deeply, too, and ultimately provide deep comfort. This is no superficial nurture course, but I do believe it reflects the heart of God for Christians to take things much more seriously as we seek to reach out into our hurting world. For us to do that effectively we need to look at some of the issues in our lives very seriously. As church members take up the challenge of working through these Steps, I believe we will see the atmosphere within congregations change significantly. No longer will leaders have to "walk on eggshells" around certain members, afraid of their likely reactions. No longer will certain members be "written off" as chronically damaged.

Also, no longer will there be frustrated and disappointed church members who have been told to "just pray" about their significant problems, but who have received no apparent answers from God.

By following these Steps, we have seen individuals set free in dynamic ways. In St John's we have people who once were seriously addicted now working as leaders. We have seen people who suffered from chronic low self-esteem now holding their heads high. We have seen those with inner pain released: they now have an open face and laughing disposition. We have seen the scared become bold and the calculating become refreshingly carefree.

Although the benefit to the individual is immense, there is a greater issue here. I believe God wants his church ready and equipped to take up the challenge of seeking his kingdom in this twenty-first century. Christians have a God-given commission to go and make disciples. Romans 12:1–2 sums up what we have experienced. Many have offered their bodies "as living sacrifices" to the Lord, and then found that by the "renewing" of their minds they no longer "conform... to the pattern of this world". Instead, they experience the healing that enables them to know God's "good, pleasing and perfect will" for the future. God then reveals his purpose for them as individuals – and also as members of groups and congregations, and as part of the whole church for the area.

Step 1 *We admit we are powerless over our sin – that our lives have become unmanageable*

So then, the law is holy, and the commandment is holy, righteous and good.

Did that which is good, then, become death to me? By no means! But in order that sin might be recognised as sin, it produced death in me through what was good, so that through the commandment sin might become utterly sinful.

We know that the law is spiritual; but I am unspiritual, sold as a slave to sin. I do not understand what I do. For what I want to do I do not do, but what I hate I do. And if I do what I do not want to do, I agree that the law is good. As it is, it is no longer I myself who do it, but it is sin living in me. I know that nothing good lives in me, that is, in my sinful nature. For I have the desire to do what is good, but I cannot carry it out. For what I do is not the good I want to do; no, the evil I do not want to do – this I keep on doing. Now if I do what I do not want to do, it is no longer I who do it, but it is sin living in me that does it.

So I find this law at work: When I want to do good, evil is right there with me. For in my inner being I delight in God's law; but I see another law at work in the members of my body, waging war against the law of my mind and making me a prisoner of the

*law of sin at work within my members. What a wretched man I
am! Who will rescue me from this body of death? Thanks be to
God – through Jesus Christ our Lord!*

*So then, I myself in my mind am a slave to God's law, but in
the sinful nature a slave to the law of sin.*

Romans 7:12–25

There are very few people who would come right out and
say, "I am powerless." However, when alcoholics begin the
path of recovery through Alcoholics Anonymous they have
to admit their powerlessness over alcohol. In fact, when
speaking at a meeting they would say, "My name is... and I
am an alcoholic." But what does this have to say to
Christians? We may not have a problem with drink. We
may not see ourselves addicted to anything, in fact. Yet the
Bible teaches us right from the start, way back in Genesis,
that in fact human beings are powerless over something.
That something is sin.

In Genesis 3 we read of God present with Adam and Eve
in the Garden of Eden. However, also present was a crafty
being who suggested to Adam and Eve an alternative to following the ways of God.

Adam had been told that he was free to eat from any
tree in the garden except from the tree of the knowledge of
good and evil. If he did, he would die (Genesis 2:17). The
serpent countered this by asking Eve whether God really
said they should not eat from *any* tree in the garden
(Genesis 3:1). Already the serpent was casting doubt on
what God had actually said by misquoting him. When the
woman reiterated God's command, the serpent then went
on to lie, or at least deliver the half truth, "You will not
surely die" (Genesis 3:4). Rather, he said, she would have
her eyes opened and know what was good and what was evil
(Genesis 3:5).

In this picture we see a choice offered to, and ultimately made by, the man and the woman. That choice was whether to follow God's command or to follow what the serpent, Satan, portrayed as truth. It was a choice of, "Who's going to be in control here?" Both Adam and Eve made that decision – it wasn't just the woman! Then they found they had done something that shifted the whole of their world view. They had decided that they would be in control.

This was fundamental to their life and had an immediate effect. For the first time they realized they were naked. Shame came upon them, they covered themselves and hid from the presence of God. We also seek to be in control of our own lives and many people also suffer similar consequences of feelings of shame and guilt. Likewise, we experience the discomfort of God's presence knowing that we have often chosen to go a different path from that commanded in his word.

We cannot blame it all on Adam and Eve, because we still personally make the same choices. We make wrong decisions daily.

Who is in control?

If we are asked, "Who is in control of your life?", what is our answer? Those of us who have been Christians for many years know that we have asked Jesus to come into our lives by his Spirit "to control us". Yet we still recognize that selfish streak in ourselves. So often we find ourselves acting self-centredly and cannot quibble with the title of "sinner", however old-fashioned it may sound. We know we do not obey God's commands all the time. We choose to go our own way even when we know God's way is better. We have to admit that we actually enjoy being selfish at times. We often want to do our own thing. We want to send God out of the room for a while.

Satan, when he was an angel, had said, "I don't want to be under your control, God. I want to have my own kingdom." As he set himself up against God, he was in effect saying, "I am now the king. I am in control." He then encouraged men and women to think in the same way so that we became little kings in our own kingdoms, in our own lives. Satan still has the mission on earth to corrupt men and women and to encourage them to take control of their own lives in rebellion to God (Ezekiel 28:12b–17 and Revelation 12:7–17).

It doesn't take much analysis of our world situation to see that making the wrong choice, by not letting God control our lives, is the major root of the world's ills. The truth is that human beings have never consistently made good choices on their own. Taking control leads to pride and many other resultant sins. In effect we have messed up our own lives and we have messed up the world in which we live. We have hurt and been hurt. We have suffered the consequences.

Outside our church we have a "wayside pulpit". It is well known in the area, as it is highly visible from a major road. One of the most talked about posters was "Hurt people hurt people." When people get hurt, then they also hurt others and the pain and the sin increases.

Commentators differ in their interpretation of Romans 7. Paul seems to speak out of anguish about his own situation. Some have said he is talking of that time before he was converted on the road to Damascus. However, the majority see it as a heart-felt cry regarding his situation after conversion. Although God's Spirit was in him and changing him, he still found himself powerless to live the way God wanted him to. "I do not understand what I do. For what I want to do I do not do, but what I hate I do" (Romans 7:15). Or, "For what I do is not the good I want to do; no, the evil I do not want to do – this I keep on doing" (verse 19). This is a graphic description of the turmoil that goes on inside us even as Christians. We do have the desire to go God's way but sin living inside us often wins out. All the good intentions in the world do not give us the power to put them into practice. No wonder Paul described himself as "a slave to sin" (verse 14). He cries, "What a wretched man I am!" (verse 24).

What we are talking about here is a deeper disease than a decision to commit an individual sin. We are talking about an attitude, our natural propensity to evil, to rebel against God. Paul always experienced this struggle of choice and control. After 35 years of being a Christian, I too am still familiar with this inclination towards rebellion.

Step 1 tackles this problem head on. It asks Christians to admit, "we are powerless over our sin – that our lives are unmanageable." It should be easy to take that step of admission if we recognize addiction as part of our lives. But the truth is that it is a huge battle for those who are addicted actually to take this first step.

The many people from an addictive background whom I have spoken to invariably say that this first step was very difficult to take. To admit that they were powerless seemed more like a pole vault than a step! Even if we have not come from an addictive background, this step is no easier to take. We think our lives are all right and yet we have to agree with Paul that we do the evil that we do not intend.

Is our life really unmanageable? You only have to watch the TV soap operas for a week to see the catalogue of disasters in so many people's lives. This may not exactly reflect our own lives, but it is not far from many people's experience. There is debt, adultery, lust, anger, violence, revenge, greed... the list goes on endlessly. It is my experience as a leader of a local church that many within our membership also exhibit signs of this inner and outer turmoil.

How do we feel?

Perhaps a good way to test this truth is to ask the question, "How do we feel?" If things are not quite right in our lives certain feelings are likely to spring up. We probably don't take much notice of them day by day unless they get extreme. However, these feelings may well trigger us to think about these fundamental questions for our lives: "Who is in control?", "Are we really powerless?", "Are our lives unmanageable?" These feelings may be one or more of the following:

- *How about loneliness?* You can be in a big room with lots of people and yet still feel lonely. If your church serves coffee after the service then look around for those who are lonely. But it's not necessarily – or only – that person on their own in the corner. Some people who are continually lonely spend much of their time talking to other people. It isn't a matter of the number of people talked to or the length of time spent with someone, it's the intense feeling of loneliness inside. That may be caused by a deeper problem.

- *Then what about the excessive need for excitement?* Some people need a buzz in their lives at all times. They need a thrill to keep them going. Many Christians suffer from this too. They need another, more exciting, meeting to go to. For them, Sunday morning services are OK but they want a more thrilling experience, a more spine-tingling encounter with God. They have something inside that needs satisfying, that really is insatiable.

- *Does anger rise up, sometimes for no real apparent reason?* It is always amazing for people to see someone explode in anger quite out of proportion to whatever provoked the reaction. Some people describe this as a sense of having to keep a volcano capped. However, it is impossible to do so at all times and occasionally the eruption takes place. Some underlying pressure needs sorting out.

- *Are there feelings of shame?* I have often met people who do not feel good about themselves. They are very self-conscious. They have little self-esteem. Sometimes people try to compensate for these inner feelings by inappropriate actions such as denigrating those around them or "being the life and soul of the party". Yet the secret feeling remains.

- *What about lying?* In order to remain in control, often we tell small lies, or sometimes even big ones. Also, one lie leads to another. The cover-up becomes more complex as we try to make it complete. Our fear, or pride, is too strong to allow us to live the truth. Jonathan Aitken, the well-known British politician who ended up in prison for perjury, recalls how this happened to him:

> The way I saw it in those early days was that the *Guardian* and Granada had published massive falsehoods about me in the areas of pimping, arms dealing and corrupt dependency on (Saudi Arabian) Prince Mohammed. In defending myself with much prideful anger against this onslaught of very serious allegations, I needed to present a seamless web of rebuttal. If that meant telling a lie about the relatively unimportant matter of who paid my £900 Ritz Hotel bill, it seemed to me to be a necessary small one in self-defence against much greater falsehoods. I therefore rode roughshod over all those rules and axioms about how the end does not justify the means; how two wrongs do not make a right; and how the truth is absolute... This was to prove a supreme act of folly.[1]

- *Do those in authority create a sense of fear?* Some people are inordinately afraid of authority figures. Their response is not thought out but is a gut reaction. They have feelings of questioning, distrust and rebellion. There could be a past hurt being expressed in present reactions.

- *Maybe there are hardly any feelings at all?* Some people in effect have suffered a "loss of feeling". The mechanism they have used to blot out pain also blots out joy. They do such a good cover-up job on a painful episode in their past that they are anaesthetized to all feelings. That person has become numb.

- *Is there a sense of unreality?* These people have a wrong view of their life. They say, "My life will be better when…" Such people often live in turmoil with various signs that life is unmanageable, for instance through debt, broken relationships or loss of work. However, they believe that their life will be better when… "When my children leave home, then I'll be at peace." "When I have a holiday." "When I'm with a new set of people as I don't really get on with my existing friends." "When I move to this new job." "When I move to this new house." "When I move to another church." Some people do go through their lives waiting for things to get better and always believing that they will… "when". However, it is an illusion and a sign of a deeper problem that is not changed by the new circumstance. The problem is part of the person.

How does this feel? Of course, some of us do make a better job of our lives than others. Some of us have been forced to confront some of our inner problems in our early years of being a Christian. However, it is my experience that many church members cope with such inner turmoil rather than see victory over it. Step 1 is about seeing victory. It is the first Step. It is the Step of admitting we are powerless, and that we need help.

Do we have any symptoms?

What symptoms do we have? At this stage some people will react by saying that none of this applies to them: "I'm sorted." But was Paul unique or is his experience actually a reflection of our situation as well? Of course, some of us have dealt with many issues in our past and we do not need to keep on going back to things that have been prayed through, healed and resolved. However, before we come too quickly to the conclusion that we are OK it is worth seeing if some of the effects common to these afflictions appear in our lives. Are the symptoms of the inner feelings there to be seen?

- *Do we seek to take more and more control?* For instance, if we have an inner anger, we will build a defence system that can spot very early a dangerous situation that may provoke this anger to erupt. We prepare ourselves, perhaps by rehearsing a response or, more radically, moving ourselves out of the situation altogether. Nevertheless, occasionally we will be taken by surprise. I can remember a situation in a previous church when a lady erupted in anger to a question which actually related to a member of her family but could, incidentally, have questioned the lady's self-worth. It caught her by surprise and the eruption had happened before she could put a lid on it. She was known to be someone who was "prickly" but not for demonstrable anger. This time her control had slipped.

- Another reaction to this inner powerlessness may well be to *take alternative action*. This invariably ends up in addictive behaviour, as the action is taken to relieve deep pain. It is rare to find someone who is addicted to a substance or behaviour pattern who does not also have some of the feelings listed above. The addiction so often is a cover-up of the pain. You have pain so you get drunk. It takes that pain away for a while. In our church project to help people with addictions, we are well aware that taking heroin makes a lot of people feel good. Getting drunk makes a lot of people feel good. Looking at pornography arouses excitement. However, the release is temporary, as the deep pain, such as loneliness or anger, does not go away for good.

- It is interesting to note that in church circles there are some *acceptable addictions*. It is not unusual to find people who are workaholics. Often they include the vicar or minister! Truthfully I have to say this has never been my problem; some say I suffer from the opposite! But I have seen many church leaders who do overwork. The question here is what does the addictive activity cover up? Some soul searching is necessary to find out that what we thought was zeal for the Lord is in effect a dissatisfaction with who we are in Christ, or an unwillingness to have space in our life that would give us time to deal with the pain of past experience.

- *Are we content?* There is much biblical teaching about peace being present in our lives no matter what busyness we experience. Peace is a fruit of the Spirit in Galatians 5. Christ himself is our peace (Ephesians 2:14). We can know the peace of God that transcends all understanding (Philippians 4:7). We can know the peace of

Christ rule in our hearts (Colossians 3:15). But we do not always feel this peace and contentment.

- Then there is the question of *relationship problems*. This is not just those outside the church. More and more Christians are having family problems or marital problems. Why is this? Often it betrays the inner turmoil and pain still present in their lives.

- Another symptom of inner problems can be the *inability to cope with criticism*. Some people have an acute radar system that picks up anything negative that could possibly reflect upon them. For these people, praise can be heaped upon them but it is largely like water off a duck's back. The slightest negative is taken to heart. Such a person does not like anyone trying to control them; there's no way they want to be under someone else's direction. They will fight that. I can think of a lady who gives off a "vibe" that in effect says, "Will you dare to talk to me?" In effect, there is no way that such a person can be appeased, as any conversation leaves open the possibility for something to be seen as a criticism or slight. Not to talk to them is in itself a slight. The consequence is that the person comes to "know" that no one really likes them.

- One symptom of some of this inner turmoil can be the *inability to keep to the rules*. Many of us make rules and then break them. For example, I try to take my role seriously as a husband and father and will at times come up with rules showing that I am in control. For instance, "For the rest of the month we are spending no more money!" This is communicated to my wife. There are also good reasons for the rule: we are nearly broke. Yet the next week I find myself buying that new pair of trousers or that new fleece. For me, that's different. I needed to spend that money. I made the rules but then did not live up to them.

- *Then there is failure.* I do try but I keep on failing in one way or another. "I will be home for tea at 5.30 p.m. without fail." But I'm not. I even find myself lying to cover up for my failure.

- A more radical symptom of inner problems can be specific action taken to escape the need for change in some way. People who have been part of the 12 Step Programme sometimes call this *doing a geographical*. It stems out of the feeling that "life will get better when..." I recall one person who, after receiving much prayer ministry for things that he had done in his life and hurts he had experienced, needed a long period of help to develop new habits based on the freedom he had received. Before the healing had really sunk in, he succumbed to the temptation to "do a geographical". Instead of the hard slog of building new habits, he and his wife felt "called" by God to join another church. It is sad to recount that this person is still bouncing around fellowships to this day.

- Finally, the inner turmoil can have specific *physical* symptoms in people's lives. Not all physical afflictions are easily explained by our doctor. For instance, ailments relating to the bladder, stomach, heart or head can be "stress related". A doctor once said to me that stress will come out in the "top, tum or ticker". Whereas some suffer from headaches, others will have stomach upsets or heart problems. There may be real medical causes, or other physical reasons for this stress – too much work, for instance – but one cause may be related to inner turmoil. What is going on inside us affects our lives and we find ourselves in physical pain. What do we do with that pain? We try and take control. We have got to sort it out. Often this is self-defeating, as the stress of trying to deal with the feelings that have provoked our stress makes matters worse.

The first Step – no easy Step

Step 1 invites us to "admit we are powerless – that our lives are unmanageable". Whatever level you find yourself at – whether you have obvious identification with some of the feelings related here or the effects described, or you just recognize your propensity to sin – the solution is to take this step of admission that we are powerless to sort our lives out on our own. Paul wrote that he was powerless to do what he wanted to do, and he did what he didn't want to do. You know that is true. We are powerless to change that. We are powerless, that is, unless we find some power other than ourselves who can take control of our lives.

Don't forget the second part of the statement in Step 1: "that our lives are unmanageable". Can we really admit that? It is so easy for us to try to say, "Look at my life, God, I hope you are pleased with it." Recently I was reading that many businesses in Britain in the early 1990s failed not because of lack of orders or the performance of the workers, but because of poor management. Wrong decisions were made. Calculated risks were not taken. There was inadequate investment. As Christians, we must not be so arrogant as to say that we can manage our lives well enough to meet God's standards and his productivity targets. God wants to do much more in us and through us. The question is whether we will hand over the management of our lives to him.

Jesus is called the Lord Jesus Christ. In our pain we need to seek Jesus as the Christ, as the Saviour who will meet us in our pain, lift us from the pit and put our feet on the rock. We admit that we are powerless and he is the Saviour.

However, Jesus is also the Lord. But before he can be Lord of our lives, there has to be some awareness and acceptance from us that we cannot manage our lives by ourselves. We do have to hand over control.

In this first step we are looking at fundamentals. Are we admitting these things to God? Some of these things may have touched you because you know there is something wrong inside you. Don't shake it off; just think of where we started with the picture of Adam and Eve and the serpent in Eden. Beware of wrongly blaming others for your situation or indeed for the way you feel. Remember when talking with God, Adam blamed Eve and Eve blamed the serpent and "he didn't have a leg to stand on!" Maybe we are in a spiritual battle and there is someone who is seeking our downfall, but in reality the buck still stops with us. We have to take responsibility for our lives and paradoxically that means in the beginning "admitting we are powerless – that our lives are unmanageable".

A prayer:

Lord, I pray that I might indeed be free, that I might not be a slave to sin but might be your slave, your servant, Lord God. Thank you that you do come, Jesus Lamb of God, to take away the sin of the world. Thank you that you included my sin. Thank you that you take away the effects of that sin as well. Change my life, Lord. Give me faith, give me honesty, so that where I see I have problems I may turn to you and admit that I am powerless and that my life is unmanageable without you, Lord. Come to me I pray, in Jesus' name. Amen.

Taking the 1st Step

Step 1. We admit we are powerless over our sin – that our lives have become unmanageable.

Step 1 is a call to honesty and then action. So, ask yourself the following questions. It would be good to record your thoughts/answers in a notebook.

1. Who is in control of your life?
    Read again what Paul writes in Romans 7:12-25 (pp. 15–16). Can you identify with this? Are you willing to admit that (no matter what best intentions you may have) you have sinned, you do sin, and you will continue to sin?

2. How does it feel to live your life?
    Can you identify with any of the following:

    Loneliness; need for excitement; anger; shame; lying; fear of authority; sense of unreality; recurring fears; resentments; guilt; sadness; self-pity; pain about situations, people or thoughts; jealousy; numbness or lack of feelings about certain things; confusion; making "crazy" decisions.

    Does it seem virtually impossible to conquer these feelings?

3. How have you coped with effects in your life such as these?
    Do you identify with any from this list:

    Taking more control; taking alternative action; developing "acceptable" addictions (e.g. eating, smoking, TV, sex, prescribed medicines); accepting discontentment; having relationship problems; inability to cope with criticism; not keeping to the rules; encountering failure; "doing a geographical"; suffering physical problems; taking risks; making excuses; lying; exaggerating stories; justifying yourself; giving advice and trying to control where people don't really want you to.

Highlight which of these you can see in your life and also add any other "symptoms" that come to mind.

4. List the people whose behaviour irritates you and what it is they do that you cannot get them to stop doing.

5. Taking the first Step is so important as it gets to the heart of our condition. Can you now admit to yourself that you are powerless over your sin and that because of this your life has become unmanageable to some extent?

6. You may find it helpful to write out the wording of Step 1, personalizing it by putting in your name.

We come to believe that God can restore us to sanity

I cry aloud to the Lord; I lift up my voice to the Lord for mercy. I pour out my complaint before him; before him I tell my trouble.

When my spirit grows faint within me, it is you who know my way. In the path where I walk men have hidden a snare for me. Look to my right and see; no-one is concerned for me. I have no refuge; no-one cares for my life.

I cry to you, O Lord; I say, "You are my refuge, my portion in the land of the living." Listen to my cry, for I am in desperate need; rescue me from those who pursue me, for they are too strong for me. Set me free from my prison, that I may praise your name.

Then the righteous will gather about me because of your goodness to me.

Psalm 142

Paul's stark statement, "I know that nothing good lives in me, that is, in my sinful nature. For I have the desire to do what is good, but I cannot carry it out" (Romans 7:18) goes to the heart of the human condition. The context is one of desperation; Paul is crying out in his wretchedness. This is not uncommon in biblical writing and echoes the cries of many in Scripture prior to Paul. For instance, we find it in Psalm 142: "I cry aloud to the Lord; I lift up my voice to the Lord for mercy. I pour out my complaint before him; before him I tell my trouble" (verses 1 and 2). The psalmist goes on to talk of growing faint, of being in desperate need of rescue, as he views his situation as a prison (verse 7).

Many of us have lost such desperation for God and for his help. When was the last time we felt desperate for God? Maybe this cry came from the psalmist, David, because at that time his life was unmanageable. In fact, he was hiding from King Saul in a cave. His life was in great danger. But, if we know anything of David, we often hear his heartfelt cry to God just to be in a close relationship with him, no matter what his situation.

Paul takes that cry further, giving us no clue of a context for his writings in Romans 7 but rather centring on his sense of powerlessness in the face of his desire to sin. Some of the language in Psalm 142 is emotive. Not only does David speak of desperation but also of "those who pursue me". This evokes a picture of being caught and hurt. Maybe in our situation we are pursued not by people but by what lies within. No matter how I try to flee or deal with these pursuers, "they are too strong for me" and I fail.

A similar description is found in Isaiah 64:6: "All of us have become like one who is unclean and all our righteous acts are like filthy rags; we all shrivel up like a leaf, and like the wind our sins sweep us away." The writer feels he is in a void, not knowing what to do, or how to move on. However, the psalmist knows the answer – the possibility of rescue lies outside him. "I cry aloud to the Lord; I lift up my voice to the Lord for mercy" (Psalm 142:1). "It is you who know my way" (verse 3). "I cry to you O Lord; I say, 'You are my refuge, my portion in the land of the living'" (verse 5). "Listen to my cry...rescue me...set me free...that I may praise your name" (verses 6 and 7).

Am I really crazy?

Step 2 says, "We come to believe that God can restore us to sanity." Before we can come to believe this, we have to accept that there are aspects of insanity to our lives. Do we really believe we are insane? The dictionary meaning of the word "sane" is "of sound mind, not mad, moderate, sensible and wise", or "sound in mind or body, healthy, not disordered". We do not have to be admitted to the local mental hospital in order to accept that there are signs of insanity in our lives. The penetrating question is "What's it like living around you?" An intriguing element of insanity is that the insane person is usually the last person to accept that fact. I recall many years ago spending time with a member of my congregation who had come to believe that he was the reincarnation of Elijah sent to bring God's message to us all. The only reasoning that worked in the end was that Elijah should pass on the mantle of the message to Elisha, so I became Elisha while he went off for a rest in the hospital! Only later did he accept that he had been insane, in delusion. Now that is an extreme case, but many of us exhibit signs of disorder within our lives.

For example, how do we respond to questions such as these:

Do you have temper tantrums?
Do you have uncontrolled anger, with sudden outbursts?
Do you use silence as a weapon with which to hurt people?
Are you a compulsive talker?
Do you sleep too much?
Are you not able to sleep even though you are tired?
Are you able to get out of bed on a morning?
Are you continually stressed?
Do you suffer from "top, tum or ticker"?

Do you over-eat, even though you know you need to lose
weight?
Do you have excessive worries?
Are you prone to irrational fears?
Do you do something to excess, like work or drink?
Do you try and control people?
Although you desire not to do these things, do you still
carry on doing them?

God does not want us to live like this. That is not how we
are meant to be. It is not acceptable behaviour.

Looking at this list of questions may provoke the
thought that there really are elements of disorder – even
insanity – within us. All these things affect and become
part of our lives but they also affect people around us. They
are often compulsive actions, too. We say we are going to
stop, but we fail every time. It is crazy! It is also crazy to
carry on living like this when help is at hand. The challenge
for us at this point is whether we will now begin to cry
aloud to God for help.

Although the origins of Alcoholics Anonymous are
plainly Christian, the 12 Step movement has broadened out
from its Christian base. Step 2 is now worded, "We come to
believe that a Power greater than ourselves could restore us
to sanity." The founders of the 12 Step movement always
knew this to be God as revealed in Jesus. However, members of AA have relied on other powers to help them be
restored to sanity. Indeed, often the "greater power" is seen
to be the Alcoholics Anonymous meeting itself. The very
sharing of a person's powerlessness and life's unmanageability is often life-changing. The support given by others
at the meeting is powerful. In the recent film *Traffic* the
young addict acknowledges the support of those she met at
the 12 Step meeting. Consequently there are many who

come out of addiction without ever having a true faith in God. However, our Christian concern is not just about a person's addiction, but healing the human condition, the propensity to sin, the powerlessness and unmanageability of their lives. We all need life-changing healing in all aspects of our lives.

Step 2 is therefore a call to faith in God as revealed in Jesus Christ. We are to hand over full control of our lives to this God so that he can lead us into all the good things he has for us in the future.

Who is on your throne?

A fellow pastor recently gave me an illustration that graphically showed what we need to do. In Figure 1, the larger circle represents our whole life and the inner circle represents who is in control. This is our natural state, with ourselves in control of all aspects of our life – where we live, what work we do, who we marry, how we use our money, what we do in our leisure time, who our friends are, and so on. As we make decisions about these things, the consequences do not work out as we had hoped. These are the signs of unmanageability and we seem ultimately powerless in sorting them all out.

Then, as we come to believe in God and accept Jesus as our Saviour who has died to take the penalty for our sins, we actually hand control of our lives over to Jesus who will now live in us by his Spirit. He is given the place of control in our lives (Figure 2). Consequently, as we offer our lives "as living sacrifices" to God (Romans 12:1) we find him restoring us to sanity through "the renewing" of our minds (Romans 12:2). Then he starts to put our life in order and helps us to live out his plan for our life: "Then you will be able to test and approve what God's will is – his good, pleasing and perfect will" (Romans 12:2). This affects every

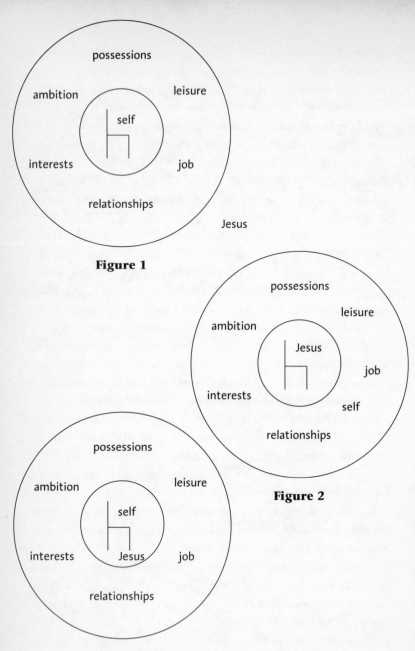

Figure 1

Figure 2

Figure 3

aspect of our life, including our relationships and how we spend our time or money.

Obviously, our old self still exists, but we have given the control of our life to the greater power, God. Even Jesus relied upon the Holy Spirit's power as he lived on earth and ministered to people (see Luke 4:1f.; Luke 4:14f.; John 5:19).

However, most of us live in the way shown by the third circle (Figure 3). Even though we have become Christians and given our lives to the Lord, at some point, often imperceptibly, we have placed our old self back in the centre, to make our decisions. Jesus is very much a part of our lives, but he is not really on the throne. This can create almost as much chaos as we knew before we became Christians. We make decisions without involving Jesus, because self is on the throne of our lives. We do what *we* want, primarily.

When we live like this we still feel it is vital that Jesus is present in our lives. But his role is now much more as an insurance policy. When things get too chaotic we have a word with him and ask for his help. If, however, we feel he is demanding too much we can push him away again. I believe that if we are really honest we will admit that this is true for much of our lives.

Most ministers have seen someone come to know God and ask him to deal with the chaos and the needs in their lives. They hand over their lives to the Lord. They ask Jesus to be their Saviour. They acknowledge him as Lord of their lives and invite the Holy Spirit to fill them and prompt them to live in his way. But, as time goes on, they begin to take back control themselves. How fickle we are! When we are desperate we will look for help, we will make promises, we will take decisive action. But then, when the desperation recedes and the aspects of pain in our lives diminish, we so often want to take back the control of our lives so that we can do what we want. We even begin to believe again that we know what is best for us.

Where's your faith?

Step 2 unsurprisingly precedes Step 3! In Step 3 we are called upon to take decisive action about handing over our wills and our lives to God. Step 2 is asking, first, whether we believe that we need restoring to sanity and, secondly, if we believe that God can do that for us. This means coming to faith in Christ. Sometimes this is a difficult step for us to take when we have a history of self-centredness and our energies have been exhausted in trying to control the chaos. It cuts right into our tightly held convictions of the need to stay in control. In fact, it demands that we take responsibility for our lives and our actions.

We can no longer blame situations or the actions of others for our chaos and pain. We acknowledge there is a power greater than ourselves that can change us. We are to believe both in God and also in his personal intervention in our lives. That is, we are to trust God and not ourselves to restore us to sanity. For some this is a process. One point at a time takes a person through the deepening of their faith.

Let us finally look at the question of restoration. In 1 Peter 5:5–11 we see that God opposes the proud but gives grace to the humble. God does want to restore us to true health in our minds, our bodies and our souls. But I don't believe he expects us to change overnight. Sanctification has never been instant. It has always been a process. But the sooner we come to "believe" the sooner we are back on the road that was first meant for us. We were created in God's image but that image has been tarnished and now God wants us to be open to his restoration work. Pride will always get in the way of God's work and humility will always enhance it.

Step 2 challenges us to take that humble step of acknowledgement that we cannot restore ourselves to sanity and we do need God to change us. Taking Step 2 destroys the foundations of pride. True humility is to know our place, which is being accepted by God for who we are and not for what we have done. As James puts it, "Humble yourselves before the Lord, and he will lift you up" (James 4:10).

A prayer:

Lord, I ask you to help me in my life as I come to Step 2. Help me to see you are our great and mighty God, that you created this whole world and yet, Lord, you stoop and draw near to me so that your power is available in my life. Lord, thank you that you are there to restore me and to bring me to sanity. I pray that you will help me to be humble. Help me to see that I need to change, that there are habits in my life that need to be broken, that there are situations in my life that have gone on for too long. Thank you that you want to bring me healing. You want to bring wholeness into my life. Lord, I am sorry that I have placed myself at the centre of my life instead of you. Please forgive me and help me to move on now with you, through Jesus Christ I pray. Amen.

Taking the 2nd Step

Step 2. We come to believe that God can restore us to sanity.

Not many of us go around saying that we are crazy! Yet there are signs of insanity in most of our lives. Once we start seeing that, we can also start to believe that God can restore us to sanity. To take this 2nd Step, ask yourself the following:

1. Have you lost a desperation for closeness with God and his rescue and freedom? See Psalm 142 (see p. 31)

2. Are you really crazy?
   Look again at the list on pp. 33–34 and see which you identify with.

3. Who is on the throne of your life?
   Look again at the figures on p. 36. Which matches your life – Figure 1 or Figure 2 or Figure 3?

4. Where's your faith?
   Do you now have the faith to see that God can restore *you* to sanity? Again, write out this 2nd Step in your notebook including your name at the beginning, personalizing it.

Step 3 — *We make a decision to turn our will and our lives over to the care of God*

When Jesus heard that John had been put in prison, he returned to Galilee. Leaving Nazareth, he went and lived in Capernaum, which was by the lake in the area of Zebulun and Naphtali – to fulfil what was said through the prophet Isaiah:

> Land of Zebulun and land of Naphtali, the way to the sea, along the Jordan, Galilee of the Gentiles – the people living in darkness have seen a great light; on those living in the land of the shadow of death a light has dawned.

From that time on Jesus began to preach, "Repent, for the kingdom of heaven is near."

As Jesus was walking beside the Sea of Galilee, he saw two brothers, Simon called Peter and his brother Andrew. They were casting a net into the lake, for they were fishermen. "Come, follow me," Jesus said, "and I will make you fishers of men." At once they left their nets and followed him.

Going on from there, he saw two other brothers, James son of Zebedee and his brother John. They were in a boat with their father Zebedee, preparing their nets. Jesus called them, and immediately they left the boat and their father and followed him.

Matthew 4:12–22

Few of us really like to be controlled. I find it intriguing to talk prospective wedding couples through the marriage service. When we get to the vows, there is invariably a reluctance on the part of the prospective wife to say she will obey her husband. I get the impression that a quick picture springs into the bride-to-be's mind showing a caveman dragging his wife behind him by her hair! Either that or a picture of the feudal lord dishing out orders to his wife and family and servants. This is far from the biblical teaching that it is the husband who carries the *responsibility* for the spiritual life of his wife and family as well as himself. The wife is being invited to come under the *protection* of that responsibility, but the fear of being *controlled* remains. I sometimes half jokingly suggest that maybe we could substitute the word obey with another. How about "submit"? In fact, that is the word given for wives in relation to their husbands in Ephesians 5:22. It is also the word given to everyone in our relationship to God. "Submit yourselves, then, to God" (James 4:7). However, to the prospective wife it sounds like "for worse" not "for better"!

It's crunch time!

Step 3 says we are to "make a decision to turn our will and our lives over to the care of God". This is decision time. We may have come to "admit we are powerless and that our lives are unmanageable" (Step 1) and "come to believe that God can restore us to sanity" (Step 2), but now it's the crunch. Will we decide to hand over our wills and our lives to the care of God?

The little booklet *Journey Into Life*, by Norman Warren[1], has been used to help many people take the step of faith and become Christians. The prayer on page 13 of this booklet has been used by thousands of people to give their lives to the Lord. It ends with some amazing statements. "Now I ask you to come into my life by your Holy Spirit. Come in as my Saviour to cleanse me, *come in as my Lord to control me* and I will serve you all the remaining years of my life *in complete obedience*." When I lead people to become Christians I discuss with them what these statements mean before they pray the prayer. Do they really want to hand over the control of their lives to God? Are they serious in wanting to obey him in the future?

Of course it needs to be explained that they will *not* be completely obedient but that is still their intention, just as the bridegroom and the bride will not fulfil their marriage vows even though they intend to. They will not always truly love each other, they will not always be patient with each other, they will not always be kind to each other, they may well be rude at times, they may well be self-seeking and self-ish, they probably will have rows and lose their tempers, and they may not always forgive each other straight away. (See 1 Corinthians 13:4–8 for the description of true love.) However, it is the wedding couple's *intention* to love each other and they state it publicly and to each other before God.

What is your God like?

So Step 3 asks if we have decided to hand over our will and our lives to the care of God? Of course, if you are a Christian you must have done this. But experience shows that a couple of penetrating questions need to be asked.

The first is, do you have the right God? Keith Miller in his book, *A Hunger for Healing*[2], tells the story of a man who was new to the 12 Step Programme and who was talking to an old-timer about the third Step.

> The man said, "No way I'm going to turn my life over to God. He would ruin me and I would deserve it." He went on to say that for him God was a giant policeman and the man's life

had been such that his experience with the police was not at all positive. The old-timer, a strong, quiet man, listened to the new man's description of God and then in all seriousness said, "You ought to fire that God. You ought to fire him. You've got the wrong God for this programme, friend. The God who operates here is loving, forgiving, and gives you all the chances you need to get on. He is honest and will always be there for you. I had a God like yours when I first came in here, but I had to fire him and get me a new God." "What can I do about a God if I fire mine?" the new man asked. The old-timer thought a minute, "Well," he said, "you could use mine till you get on your own feet."

People can be members of a church for many years and still have a wrong view of God and as a result have a wrong practical theology. Some in our congregation at St John's have had to shed a view of God based on unhappy experiences in the past. Some have been taught about God in such a way that their picture of him is of a vengeful being, a custodian of the rule book who is always waiting to pounce when we break a rule. He will be quick to convict and to punish. Others find it difficult to relate to God as Father. Their experience with their earthly father fills them with distrust. They have real fear born out of the pain they received through abuse, disappointment or being let down.

We need to go back to the Bible to see the true picture of the God we need for Step 3. We need to fire any other image of God and start building a new relationship with the true God as revealed in Jesus Christ. It's such a good place to start. The Gospels reveal to us just what God is like. When Philip said to Jesus, "Lord, show us the Father and that will be enough for us", Jesus answered, "Don't you know me, Philip, even after I have been among you such a long time? Anyone who has seen me has seen the Father" (John 14:8–9).

What is God like? Look at Jesus. But we must not only look in the New Testament, because the danger is that we might write off God as revealed in the Old Testament. The longer I have been a Christian, the more I have been aware of how God is revealed powerfully in the Old Testament scriptures. In fact we can understand so much about Jesus and who he is and what he is like through the Old Testament. It gives us a deeper awareness of God's love and justice.

The second question is this. Is God really your God or is he your servant? Do you see God primarily as the fifth emergency service? In Britain we acknowledge the emergency services as the police, the fire brigade, and the ambulance service and, in recent years, advertisements tell us that the Automobile Association is the fourth emergency service. We need to beware of treating God as an emergency service. In other words, if we cannot get things sorted out ourselves then we will go to God to sort it out but only as a last resort.

So is God the Lord of your life or is he there as an insurance policy, someone to get you out of trouble? When we begin a new project, we consult all the experts we can find. When my church began a project to help those who were dependent on drugs we talked to social workers, drug workers, those running rehabilitation centres, probation officers, and former drug addicts. But first of all we talked with God to discern his will on this, even though the need was so evident. It would have been totally unacceptable to go ahead with the project and then ask God to bail us out when we found ourselves in trouble later.

To go the way of our will and ask God to bless it is the path to disappointment. I remember a man who started attending our church. He looked about 60 although he was only 44. He had a drink problem and came to admit that he was powerless and his life was unmanageable. He came to faith in the belief that God could restore him to sanity. However, the stumbling block was here in Step 3. The man wanted to follow his own will, which was the wish to "drink like a gentleman", a phrase well known in AA circles. This meant he did not want to give up drinking. He just did not want drinking to ruin his life. However, for him that appeared not to be an option. I have no doubt that God could have restored him to sanity and would have done so, but he needed this man's will to be given over to him first. It is sad to record that he has since died. Only God knows if he ever made that decision. Perhaps we see here a parallel to the rich young ruler who came to Jesus and turned away, wanting to hang on to his riches (Luke 18:18–30).

It is so dangerous never to seek God's will first but only to ask him to bless what we want to happen. There is a big difference. Prayer is hearing from God what he wants us to say back to him, for him then to do.

And the good news is…!

The Gospel, the good news of Jesus, has been the same from the beginning. Matthew states that the coming of Jesus was a light shining in the darkness (Matthew 4:16). As Jesus preached, he called people to repent. He was looking for that admission that we had left God's plan for our lives and had gone our own way. The repenting was not just sorrow for what had gone wrong but the specific act of turning away from the actions and attitudes of the past and handing over our wills to him.

When Jesus met the first disciples he said to them, "Come, follow me." But he also said, "I will make you fishers of men" (Matthew 4:19). In simple terms, that meant he had plans for each and every disciple just like he does for us. God wants to make us of use to himself and others in the building of his kingdom. But he needs us to come to him and he needs us to follow him. Step 3 is about this decision to follow him. The disciples wasted no time: their reaction was instantaneous. "Immediately they left the boat and their father and followed him." They recognized someone in Jesus that they could trust and who had the answers to their need. I wonder how much they were also struck by his promise of having plans for their lives.

Finally, let's get practical. How do we actually do Step 3? On the surface it seems easy because all we really need to do is pray a simple prayer handing over our will and our lives to God. But hold on a minute! Before we do that we need to know that taking Step 3 has consequences.

Step 3 leads to the other Steps

In AA circles there is something known as "the 12 Step waltz". It goes a bit like this – *one two three, one two three, one two three, one two three...* This has proved to be the experience of many people who have taken these steps in the past. They make a decision to take Step 3. They do it. They hand over control of their will and their life to God. But then what?

For example, when you make a decision to buy a car that's not the end of it. It's just the start. You then have to think about the price range, the size, the insurance implications, the colour, the extras, the part-exchange value of your existing car, the tax implications – the list goes on. Making a decision to buy a house can be even more complicated. I remembered everything when I first bought a house except to contact the electricity company, so we spent our first night in the dark! So the decision in Step 3 has consequences. It is the beginning of Steps 4 to 12. Some people, however, never fully realize this and just stop there, thinking all will be sorted. They get no further, and some months or years later they have to start again at Step 1.

The fact is, Step 3 is a decision also to do Steps 4 to 12; not to do the one-two-three, one-two-three waltz. Many people don't manage to continue. They keep on giving their lives to Jesus, they give him control, they say the words, but they end there. They do not live out the rest of the Steps.

It is relatively easy to say, "I give my will and my life to the Lord now." But to be ready to do that we have to clear up the past and we have to work out the future and we have to deal with it in the present. It means doing that now. God does not wave a magic wand over us to take away our histories. Yes, we do become a new creation and "the old has gone, the new has come" (2 Corinthians 5:17). But this is to be a process on our part. As we bring our past before the Lord, its negative power over us will be taken away.

I wonder how guilty we have been in recent years by offering a slick, quick conversion experience? The eighteenth-century preacher John Wesley insisted that a person's repentance prayer had detail in it: what sins had been committed and when and to whom. Then he taught his class members to be willing to give details of their sin at the weekly meeting. Lawrence Singlehurst of Youth With a Mission teaches the necessity for young people of today to give details when repenting, as they can absorb our postmodern dualism, happy to be a Christian on a Sunday night and to take drugs and sleep around during the week.

So, as we take Step 3 are we willing to begin the process of allowing our lives to come under God's microscope? Are we ready to make a complete and clean breast of our lives to date? This includes attitudes and habits as well as actions.

A prayer:
   Dear Lord, thank you for this journey that I am on. Maybe I don't understand quite what it all means but I can trust you to

lead me. I acknowledge before you that it's not just about making some promise today but it's about some actions I must take in the future. Thank you for those fishermen all those years ago who did not really know what it meant to follow you, Lord Jesus, and yet they took the risk. Thank you that they followed you through thick and thin, that they were challenged to the depth of their being and they stuck with you and they reaped the benefits. Thank you for their example of finding freedom and being filled with the Spirit. Lord, I pray that you will help me to do the same things today that they did then: to immediately leave my past and follow you. Lord, help me this day to hand over control of my will and my life to you, to your care, because of the loving God that you are. I praise your name, Lord God. Amen.

Taking the 3rd Step

Step 3. We make a decision to turn our will and our lives over to the care of God.

In Step 3 we are not only asking God to come and sort out our lives, we are deciding that it is best if he controls our lives. So it's decision time. Are you now ready to take this Step?

1. First you need to ask yourself the following questions:

   (a) Have you the right God? Is he God as revealed in Jesus and in the Bible?
   (b) What do you *feel* when you consider putting your life and will, your whole future, in God's hands? Do you have any specific fears? Especially consider whether you can really trust God.
   (c) Is God really your Lord or is he your servant? Do you see him no longer just as Saviour for you but also as Lord of your life?

(d) Just as Jesus called his disciples to follow him, there is now a personal calling for you. Do you see how personal this calling is for you? How do you feel about it?

(e) Have you fully realized that taking Step 3 means you are promising to take the following Steps 4–12? The first disciples made a decision to follow Jesus, but they then had to live out that decision in action over the rest of their lives.

2. Write down the wording of Step 3, personalizing it by beginning "I... (your name) make a decision to turn my will and my life over to your care, God."

Step **4**   *We make a*
searching and
fearless moral
inventory of
ourselves

Let us examine our ways and test them, and let us return to the Lord. Let us lift up our hearts and our hands to God in heaven, and say: "We have sinned and rebelled and you have not forgiven.

"You have covered yourself with anger and pursued us; you have slain without pity. You have covered yourself with a cloud so that no prayer can get through. You have made us scum and refuse among the nations.

"All our enemies have opened their mouths wide against us. We have suffered terror and pitfalls, ruin and destruction." Streams of tears flow from my eyes because my people are destroyed.

My eyes will flow unceasingly, without relief, until the Lord looks down from heaven and sees. What I see brings grief to my soul because of all the women of my city.

Those who were my enemies without cause hunted me like a bird. They tried to end my life in a pit and threw stones at me; the waters closed over my head, and I thought I was about to be cut off.

I called on your name, O Lord, from the depths of the pit. You heard my plea: "Do not close your ears to my cry for relief." You came near when I called you, and you said, "Do not fear."

O Lord, you took up my case; you redeemed my life.
Lamentations 3:40–58

Let's face it!

In Lamentations 3 we read, "Let us examine our ways and test them, and let us return to the Lord." That verse sums up Step 4. However, the passage goes on to give a good description of how we feel when we are having problems. We feel that God has in fact "covered himself with anger and pursued us", he has blocked himself away in a cloud so he doesn't hear our prayers. We sense he is not doing anything and we are suffering the consequences. The word-pictures are graphic descriptions of how it feels: terror, pitfalls, ruin and destruction, and "the waters closed over my head, and I thought I was about to be cut off" (verse 54).

In the midst of the anguish there is the acknowledgement that "we have sinned and rebelled" (verse 42). But there is also the cry of hope: "I called on your name, O Lord, from the depths of the pit. You heard my plea... You came near when I called you, and you said, 'Do not fear.' O Lord, you took up my case; you redeemed my life" (verses 55–58).

This challenges us to ask if we similarly cry out to God and now take this fundamental step towards healing. Step 4 is so important. It requires action. We are to "make a searching and fearless moral inventory of ourselves". This is the outworking of the decision made in Step 3. We are trying to sort out our lives ourselves, but we have had to say that we can't and that we need God to come to us and change us. But Step 4 is, I believe, God's plan for us. This is not primarily about *justification* (being right with God) but it is about *sanctification* (becoming more like God). That is, moving on in Christian life; living out our new freedom; and experiencing life in all its fullness. It is about living in God's good, perfect and pleasing will, and being available to him to "shine like stars in the universe" (Philippians 2:15).

Do we really need to do this?

A big problem for many Christians is that we do not think we need to do this. It's a bit drastic, it's a bit over the top. In the Anglican church, part of the weekly service is the "general confession". People say they are sorry for their sins. We may give a little detail by saying, "we have sinned in thought, word and deed". But this is a general confession, not a specific confession, not a once and for all confession to do with our past life as we make a deep repentance. It is not a complete turning away from our past life to experience God's new life for us.

A young man whom I will call Glen once had a dramatic experience of God while walking down a street in Bradford. He subsequently got to know Christians and was baptized. But his past still haunted him and it was only five years later, when he began to look at his life and make a moral inventory, that he began to receive healing and freedom.

We start with *our sins* and take responsibility for what we have said, thought or done specifically. There are also sins that need to be entered in our moral inventory that we have committed only in response to what others have done or said to us. We will look at those and the hurt experienced by us in Step 4$^{1}/_{2}$.

People who have been Christians for some time (and I have been a Christian for 35 years) will readily say that they have done this before. But beware. How often do we suffer the consequences of guilt for actions of the past? The late David Watson used to illustrate this by saying we place our sins in a bin and ask God to come and take them away. But before God gets a chance to come (as the refuse collector) we go back to look in the bin and sometimes even get the sin out again. We can't leave it alone. We feel guilty still.

Obviously, if we have done the equivalent of Step 4 in the past we should not need to be doing it again. If we have done it once then God has forgiven us and he has set us free and we need to move on. We need particularly to be putting Steps 5 to 12 into practice. But if it is some time since we last did this Step then we need to make sure we have not stored up a new accumulation of sins that have not been dealt with in detail.

Jesus asks us to do Step 4!

I am sometimes asked why we need to go into this detail. What's the biblical backing for it? My answer is: let us look at what Jesus did. Immediately after calling the disciples ("Come, follow me... I will make you... "), he preached his Sermon on the Mount (Matthew 5–7). This sermon prompts us to look seriously at our lives. The message is that Christians should be salt and light in this decaying and dark world. Jesus was asking whether we *are* salt and light. Step 4 gives us a chance to hold up our hands and admit where we are wrong. Look at some of the key points of Jesus' sermon.

Murder (Matthew 5:21–26). Jesus said, "You have heard that it was said to the people long ago, 'Do not murder, and anyone who murders will be subject to judgment.' But I tell you that anyone who is angry with his brother will be subject to judgment." Jesus' words are very penetrating. We may hide behind the commandment "Do not murder" because we say, "I have never murdered anyone." But actually there is anger in our heart. Later on, in Matthew 15:19, Jesus talks about how anger and other bad things come out of our hearts.

This passage points the finger at the way we think as well as at our actual deeds. I have never murdered anyone, but I have felt anger. Step 4 asks if we are going to repent of it. Are we going to write it down? Are we going to deal with the anger we feel against certain people? What about the resentment and the fear involved? When was the event exactly? Who was it about? What was our part in it?

Adultery (Matthew 5:27–30). Jesus says, "You have heard that it was said, 'Do not commit adultery.' But I tell you that anyone who looks at a woman lustfully has already committed adultery with her in his heart. If your right eye causes you to sin, gouge it out and throw it away. It is better for you to lose one part of your body than for your whole body to be thrown into hell. And if your right hand causes you to sin, cut it off and throw it away." Jesus' message here goes beyond adultery to the whole question of sexual attitudes. I have often heard people say, "Well I do have a small problem with sex." Actually they have a big problem, but they call it a little problem because it's hidden. What God is asking us to do in Step 4 is to write down all that we can remember that is wrong in this area.

Which of the following form part of your history? Suggestive language, suggestive actions, casual sex, adultery, flirting, thinking, doing, rape, using sex as a weapon (particularly in marriage), dishonesty about your feelings, imagined affairs (it's all in the head), excuses, lies, resentment, hatred, revenge (I'll make him pay), justifying (I can't help it; she/he made me). Admittedly we are bombarded by sexual images throughout the day and particularly by advertising. But we do have to take responsibility for our thoughts, words and actions.

Of all areas of sin, this is the one we are often most reluctant to write down and confess. It is so very difficult to admit to ourselves and to God and indeed to some other person the extent of our sexual sin. But let's be honest. Most of us have sinned in some way sexually, particularly men. When I took Step 4 and had to admit to another man my sexual sins of the past it did not seem to come as much of a surprise to him. Indeed, he later confessed similar sins of his own. We are sexual beings who are fallen. We face a battle and often we lose it because we keep our sin secret and never know the true forgiveness and lifting of the shame that God has for us. We then do not enjoy the power of God in us to win the battle.

Divorce (Matthew 5:31–32). Jesus says, "It has been said, 'Anyone who divorces his wife must give her a certificate of divorce.' But I tell you that anyone who divorces his wife, except for marital unfaithfulness, causes her to commit adultery, and anyone who marries a woman so divorced commits adultery." Later, in Matthew 19, we find Jesus stating that the divorce certificate was only granted because of our hardness of heart. Many people's relationships are in a mess. It is not only in the TV soap operas that people have problems. They occur in real life and in the church. So what have we done wrong? We need to think through what has caused hurt and now can be seen to have been done out of selfish motives. We may try to justify ourselves because our partners or loved ones have hurt us. But in Step 4 we are not looking at them. We are looking at *our* sin. We must ask what is our part in broken or messy relationships.

Oaths/curses (Matthew 5:33–37). Jesus says, "Again, you have heard that it was said to the people long ago, 'Do not break your oath, but keep the oaths you have made to the Lord'. But I tell you, do not swear at all: either by heaven, for it is God's throne; or by earth, for it is his footstool." Sometimes oaths can in effect be curses, and curses are so powerful! When have you cursed someone else? When have you cursed yourself? When have you made an oath to yourself, for example, "I will *never* allow that to happen again, I will *never* let anyone get so close to me again, I will *never* get hurt in that way again." That's a curse. You have cursed yourself. You have made an oath and it has power. The evil one particularly likes curses. They bind us. They also put a bind upon a person if we curse them. When we say to our child, "You are stupid", that curse has power and the child often appropriates it for him or herself, doubling its power.

We need to look back to times when we have cursed others, and we need to look back at times when we have made oaths to ourselves and oaths with others. We need to repent. Often when praying with people I have found that they have been living under a curse placed upon them by someone close to them. That curse has to be broken. However, very often that person has taken hold of that curse and in a sense has cursed themselves as well. They have believed it and given it power and started living it out. Then they need to repent of it. It has become part of their moral inventory.

Revenge (Matthew 5:38–42). Jesus says, "You have heard that it was said, 'Eye for eye, and tooth for tooth.' But I tell you, Do not resist an evil person. If someone strikes you on the right cheek, turn to him the other also. And if someone wants to sue you and take your tunic, let him have your cloak as well. If someone forces you to go one mile, go with him two miles. Give to the one who asks you, and do not turn away from the one who wants to borrow from you." Revenge is such a basic instinct. We are so quick to retaliate and we often convince ourselves it is for the other person's good, to teach them a lesson. The Old Testament and New Testament teaching does hold together. The edict, "eye for eye, tooth for tooth" (Exodus 21:24) was given to the nation of Israel and has remained a principle for law in society. The punishment should fit the crime, stating a maximum punishment so that revenge would not get out of hand. But when Jesus comes to talk about personal relationships the edict is "turn the other cheek". You can see this balance of two principles demonstrated in a soccer match. One player is fouled by another and the fouled player retaliates. The referee then steps in and may well punish both players equally. Both have committed an offence. If the injured player had not retaliated then the referee would have stepped in (hopefully) and delivered punishment fitting the crime to the perpetrator. The rules of the game would have been carried out. When the injured player took the law into his own hands, trouble really started for himself as well.

How bitter are we? Do we easily get angry and retaliate? Do we harbour hatred? Do we plot and scheme for revenge? It is understandable, but sad, to see or hear the parents of children who have been abducted or murdered speaking out of bitter hatred for the perpetrators of the crime. Who is to say we would not feel the same? It is not easy to lay down the supposed "right" to revenge. It has often been said that we either get "better or bitter". It is possible that bitter people may eventually become as bad as the perpetrator of the crime that has hurt them. When we hang on to a desire for revenge we are open to all kinds of evil things.

The desire for revenge is common. It rears its head in everyday life. Think of marriages. Even though Paul's description of love in 1 Corinthians 13 includes "it keeps no record of wrongs", I have often seen a "tit for tat" attitude between couples. "If she is going to act like that, then I'll show her." I find it can be a first reaction in me in my marriage. I feel justified in desiring revenge. Nevertheless, it is wrong. It is sin.

Love for enemies (Matthew 5:43–48). Jesus says, "You have heard that it was said, 'Love your neighbour and hate your enemy.' But I tell you: Love your enemies and pray for those who persecute you." This follows the issue of revenge. But the emphasis here is on loving action. It is not just giving up the right to revenge, it is taking active steps to show love to those who are your enemies and who persecute you.

This is a hard teaching. It goes against our nature to make overtures of love towards those who we see as our enemies. And note that sometimes this includes God. He can become like an enemy in our mind, perhaps because we feel he has let us down in some way. We need to bring this into the open and repent of where we have gone wrong. We cannot get spiritually free if we hang on to such hateful attitudes.

Acts of righteousness (Matthew 6:1–4). Jesus says, "Be careful not to do your 'acts of righteousness' before men, to be seen by them. If you do, you will have no reward from your Father in heaven. So when you give to the needy, do not announce it with trumpets, as the hypocrites do in the synagogues and on the streets, to be honoured by men... But when you give to the needy, do not let your left hand know what your right hand is doing." Jesus is not just talking about giving to the needy. He is talking about issues of pride and religiosity. In other words, he is addressing thoughts like: "I am better than them"; "Fancy them doing that – I wouldn't do anything like that"; "Look at me, do you see what I am doing?"; "Come on, give me credit for what I am doing here."

A good example of this is the person who has a Christian façade – an air of superspirituality that most others know is not the real them. They are different people in church or at a cell group meeting from the people they are at work or at home. They may not even realize that they have this façade and it would help them greatly if they came to see it for themselves. We need to check if we have a problem like this. Our relationship with God should be such that we are open to him showing us what we are really like and also how he wants us to be.

Prayer (Matthew 6:5–18). Jesus leads us through teaching on prayer and fasting and provides a blueprint for the way we relate to God. We need to study this carefully and acknowledge where we have failed in our relationship with the Father and our communication with him. Again, note the warning against hypocrisy. It's not only human beings outside the church who think Christians are hypocrites! God also thinks – and knows – that we are. One of our wayside pulpit posters that got a laugh but had a serious message was "'This church is full of hypocrites.' Not true! There's always room for one more."

Money/materialism (Matthew 6:19–24). Jesus says, "Do not store up for yourselves treasures on earth, where moth and rust destroy, and where thieves break in and steal. But store up for yourselves treasures in heaven, where moth and rust do not destroy, and where thieves do not break in and steal. For where your treasure is, there your heart will be also." The question is, does money and/or materialism rule us? We live in an age in which things that once were luxuries are now necessities. Not only do we need a fridge, we also need a freezer. We need a house phone *and* a mobile phone. We don't just want a TV with a remote control, we need teletext too – and a satellite dish and interactive set-top box to link to the internet, and large screen and DVD!

In the week I was writing this, a programme on television gave a grim warning of the exhaustion of our oil supplies worldwide. It was estimated that in 20 or 30 years we would be in serious trouble, not having enough power to sustain life as we now experience it with all our "necessities". The programme went on to say that although there were alternative sources of power, estimates were that in 25 years 80% of power would still need to come from oil. How are we going to cope?

In our inventory let us get serious about how materialistic we are and how much we are ruled by money. Where do we really find our security? Quite often we are dishonest about this. We say we trust in God but when the problems come along, for instance with money, we look for all sorts of schemes and ways out rather than simply trusting in God. It is difficult for many of us to tithe, and indeed go beyond the tithe, in accordance with New Testament teaching. It may be that lack of trust (and excess greed) has caused some of the problems in the first place.

So where is our "treasure"? Is it really in our relationship with God, and do we see that all that we have is from God? Repenting of wrong dependence on money and material things is the beginning of freedom and true security.

Worry (Matthew 6:25-34). Jesus says, "Therefore I tell you, do not worry about your life." Someone said to me once that worry was a choice. Maybe I am slow but I had never actually thought of it like that before. I believed worry was something that came over me and I had no choice about it. Yet it does relate to our trust in God and questions where exactly our security lies. I need to know my worth in God, which is not based upon what I have got or what has been given to me or indeed what I have achieved. My worth is found in God's love for me and his acceptance of me.

We worry about all sorts of things. We worry about money; how we will make ends meet. Or about tomorrow: what will I do in that situation? what will I say? what will they say? Or about those around us: will they be all right? will they be kept safe? However, all this begs the question of whether we believe God is committed to us and is rooting for us, whether he will look after us, lead us and provide for us. For example, how many young people really trust God to provide them with a partner for the future? We begin saying things such as, "God's not going to get anyone for me; God's not going to provide what I need; I need to hang on to this, just in case."

Judging others (Matthew 7:1–6). Jesus says, "Do not

judge, or you too will be judged. For in the same way you judge others, you will be judged, and with the measure you use, it will be measured to you." We like to compare ourselves with others, with what they have got, what they have achieved, or how life has panned out for them. We criticize out of a spirit of superiority. Jesus says, beware. We would be in a very sorry state if God actually judged us in the way that we judge other people. Consequently, we need to repent of any judgemental attitude we have and get rid of that sin before we too appear before the judgement seat.

Becoming rock solid

I believe there is ample material in the Sermon on the Mount to show that we have not achieved perfection and that we do have a catalogue of sins to confess and repent of. I find it amazing the detail that Jesus goes into, just in one sermon! Some of the above headings, however, are just gateways to whole areas of our lives. What we are being asked to do in Step 4 is a fearless and searching moral inventory of our lives. We need to make sure we do it thoroughly. The Sermon on the Mount finishes with this very well-known passage, "Therefore everyone who hears these words of mine and puts them into practice is like a wise man who built his house on the rock. The rain came down, the streams rose, and the winds blew and beat against that house; yet it did not fall, because it had its foundation on the rock" (Matthew 7:24–25). That's what we are about: not only saying the words but doing the actions.

Can we be fearless in this? It is well known that "Do not fear" is said 366 times in the Bible, one for each day of the year, even when it's a leap year. And cowardice is revealed as a sin in Revelation 21:8. But we need to ask God for that bravery, boldness and determination to see this through. I recall a lady who told me how she had struggled to do Step 4.

I had visited the idea of using the 12 Steps in a women's cell group but I got stuck at Step 4 and found the idea too hard to deal with. I knew there was no getting away from it, God wanted me to deal with it, but I kept putting it off. Subsequently, in my quiet time at home, I looked up a reference in my Bible passage to find Isaiah 43:25–26: "I, even I, am he who blots our your transgressions... Review the past for me." I thought I had better do it there and then. I did!

This is our chance to do such a thorough stock-take of our lives that God can free us in a dramatic way to live fruitfully. Don't forget that the Sermon on the Mount also talks about good fruit (Matthew 7:17–20). God's plan for us is that we should be fruitful Christians living in abundance of life.

A prayer:

Dear Lord, I thank you and praise you that you are such a loving God. Thank you that you don't want me to sink under the weight of my sin but you want to set me free. You want to make my life manageable. You want to bring sanity back to me. You want to bring your power to me as I also experience your love. You want to change me in my will and in my life. You want to come and cleanse me and free me and forgive me, Lord God. And I pray that as I look at the details of my life you will help me to be real, help me to be open, help me to be honest with you. Help me not to shift the blame but to take the shame and see it dealt with by you. Lord God, give me your power and determination to see this through, that I might experience that release and stand before you pure and clean. In the name of our Lord Jesus Christ who died for me. Amen.

Taking the 4th Step

Step 4. We make a searching and fearless moral inventory of our-
selves.

Here we are being asked to face up to our sinfulness!
Step 4 is going beyond a general confession to a specific,
appointed and particular wiping of the slate clean.

1. Most people when they start Step 4 actually find themselves worrying about Step 5 – sharing it with another
   person. Forget about this for the moment. Face that Step
   when you get to it.

2. For starters, look through the following teaching of
   Jesus from the Sermon on the Mount. Acknowledge
   against this list where there are specific areas in your
   life you need to repent of:
   Murder (Matthew 5:21–26)
   Adultery (Matthew 5:27–30)
   Divorce (Matthew 5:31–32)
   Oaths/curses (Matthew 5:33–37)
   Revenge (Matthew 5:38–42)
   Love for enemies (Matthew 5:43–48)
   Acts of righteousness (Matthew 6:1–4)
   Prayer (Matthew 6:5–18)
   Money/materialism (Matthew 6:19–24)
   Worry (Matthew 6:25–34)
   Judging others (Matthew 7:1–6).

3. Take a moment to look back over your life and particularly try to identify areas of shame or guilt.

4. At this point ask God to help you overcome your fear and
   help you cope with any pain that may hurt you. This fear

may be of looking at some of these areas, or going into detail.

5. Begin to make a searching and fearless moral inventory of your life. You may do this by beginning with your earliest memories of sin and working towards today. Alternatively, you may want to look at particular areas of your life (as Jesus taught) and list chronologically sins you have committed in these areas down the years. When making these lists, avoid just making headings – give detail, including what was done, who was affected and what the consequences were. Ask God to bring things to memory. Most people find it helpful to do it over a few days rather than all in one go.

6. Begin to ask God whom you will share this list with in Step 5. It may be your cell group leader or it may be another member of your cell. Let God guide you. Do Step 5 now BEFORE YOU GO ON TO 4½.

Step 4½ We recognize the hurt in our lives. We forgive those who have caused it and we ask for it to be healed

You were taught, with regard to your former way of life, to put off your old self, which is being corrupted by its deceitful desires; to be made new in the attitude of your minds; and to put on the new self, created to be like God in true righteousness and holiness.

Therefore each of you must put off falsehood and speak truthfully to his neighbour, for we are all members of one body. "In your anger do not sin": Do not let the sun go down while you are still angry, and do not give the devil a foothold. He who has been stealing must steal no longer, but must work, doing something useful with his own hands, that he may have something to share with those in need.

Do not let any unwholesome talk come out of your mouths, but only what is helpful for building others up according to their needs, that it may benefit those who listen. And do not grieve the Holy Spirit of God, with whom you were sealed for the day of redemption. Get rid of all bitterness, rage and anger, brawling and slander, along with every form of malice. Be kind and compassionate to one another, forgiving each other, just as in Christ God forgave you.

Be imitators of God, therefore, as dearly loved children and

live a life of love, just as Christ loved us and gave himself up for us as a fragrant offering and sacrifice to God.

But among you there must not be even a hint of sexual immorality, or of any kind of impurity, or of greed, because these are improper for God's holy people. Nor should there be obscenity, foolish talk or coarse joking, which are out of place, but rather thanksgiving. For of this you can be sure: No immoral, impure or greedy person – such a man is an idolater – has any inheritance in the kingdom of Christ and of God. Let no-one deceive you with empty words, for because of such things God's wrath comes on those who are disobedient. Therefore do not be partners with them.

For you were once darkness, but now you are light in the Lord. Live as children of light (for the fruit of the light consists in all goodness, righteousness and truth) and find out what pleases the Lord. Have nothing to do with the fruitless deeds of darkness, but rather expose them. For it is shameful even to mention what the disobedient do in secret. But everything exposed by the light becomes visible, for it is light that makes everything visible.

Ephesians 4:22–5:14

Some explanation is needed here as we make a significant adaptation to the original 12 Steps. Step 4 mirrors exactly the original Step 4, but in this chapter, $4^1/_2$, we have added a new step, that of concentrating on events where we have been hurt by others.

This adaptation is not done lightly, but it has been found to be necessary because so many of those who have undertaken the 12 Step Programme have been held back from total freedom by the lack of healing received for damage done to them through hurtful situations.

It is not surprising that the original authors of the 12 Steps did not spend much time speaking of those hurts done to them. The addicted person is so ready to blame others and so tempted to shirk the responsibility for their actions, that to raise the whole subject of trauma introduced into their lives by others would have been likely to deflect them from the central message of accepting the blame and admitting responsibility for sins committed.

It is, of course, necessary for all of us to deal thoroughly with the sins we have committed and in no way to shirk responsibility. We must take the blame and we must come before God in repentance.

You might think that this passage from Paul's letter to the Ephesians would have been more relevant to Step 4. There is so much teaching here about practical Christian living and the need to get rid of "the fruitless deeds of darkness". But it also contains some telling phrases that are the keys to healing our hurts. "Put off your old self, which is being corrupted by its deceitful *desires*" (verse 22). "Be made new in the *attitude* of your minds" (verse 23). "Do not let the sun go down while you are *still angry*" (verse 26). "Do not give the devil a *foothold*" (verse 27). "Get rid of all *bitterness*, rage and anger" (verse 31). This is how many of us have become, and these are things we need to deal with.

There is no doubt that we need God to heal the hurt that we experience in life. He promises to "bind up the broken-hearted" (Isaiah 61:1). "For the Lamb at the centre of the throne will be their shepherd; he will lead them to springs of living water. And God will wipe away every tear from their eyes" (Revelation 7:17). However, this healing does not have to wait until eternity. It can be experienced by us here and now. Yet the key to it seems to lie with us. The only part of the Lord's Prayer that is repeated in Matthew 6 is that about forgiveness. "Forgive us our sins, as we forgive those who sin against us" (verse 12). "For if you forgive men when they sin against you, your heavenly Father will also forgive you. But if you do not forgive men their sins, your Father will not forgive your sins" (verses 14 and 15).

The trouble is that when we are hurt we usually react in a sinful way! Then so easily a blockage to our healing develops because we do not forgive those who have sinned against us and hurt us. Instead we hold onto resentment, anger and hatred.

It seems so unfair that those who have been badly hurt are asked to repent of their reaction. I recall a young woman who, in prayer ministry with myself and one of our female leaders, gave details of a horrific episode of abuse that ended in rape. Yet as we prayed it became clear that this woman had to repent of her actions, feelings and attitudes that followed the events. She had such bitterness and hatred in her. She had also placed curses on herself based on guilt and shame. So she needed God's love to surround her and his power and strength and determination to take this dramatic action of repentance. But in time she did it and the healing power of God was overwhelming to cauterize the wound that deeply affected her whole being and the way she lived. She was no longer ruled by shame. She found the deep well of anger drying up. She even started to like herself. She was different. She was carefree.

Look again at the list of injunctions from Ephesians 4 and 5: "put off your old self... be made new in the attitude of your minds... do not let the sun go down while you are still angry... do not give the devil a foothold... get rid of all bitterness, rage and anger." I am sure it was no different for the Christians in Ephesus. Why were they angry? Why did they hold bitterness? Why did they have a wrong attitude? Many of them also would have been hurt badly in their lives. Yet their reactions were not acceptable according to Paul.

Step $4^1/_2$ says, "We recognize the hurt in our lives. We

forgive those who have caused it and we ask for it to be healed." It is necessary to uncover some of the hurts that we have experienced because for many of us they are not on the surface. When someone has hurt us we try to forget it, bury it, cover it over or ignore it. Sometimes people do a complete "shut down". I have prayed with people who have no significant memory before the age of nine. Praise God that as we have prayed the Holy Spirit has revealed to them some of the hurt that they experienced in the years leading up to that time, which caused them to shut down their memories completely. On the surface of their lives it was as though these hurtful events had never happened. Yet they had left a tell-tale residue. Their lives were marred due to what they had experienced.

Beware though! We are not in the business of pressurizing people we are praying with to seek endlessly for details from those hidden areas. If there are events that need to be revealed then the Holy Spirit will reveal them.

An illustration (Figure 4) given by Dr Paul Roberts of ISAAC (The International Substance Abuse and Addiction Coalition) shows what sort of hurts we experience and also what effects they have in our lives.

Hurts in our root system

This picture of a tree with the root system showing represents our life. The root system reflects negative and positive stimuli in our life. The hurts we have experienced will be among the negatives. The positives may include such things as a sense of security due to our parents' love, encouragement we have received from many people as we grew up, or their appreciation of what we have done. However, as we are concentrating on the hurts this illustration centres mainly upon them.

Look first at *hatred*. Why is it here? It is usually because

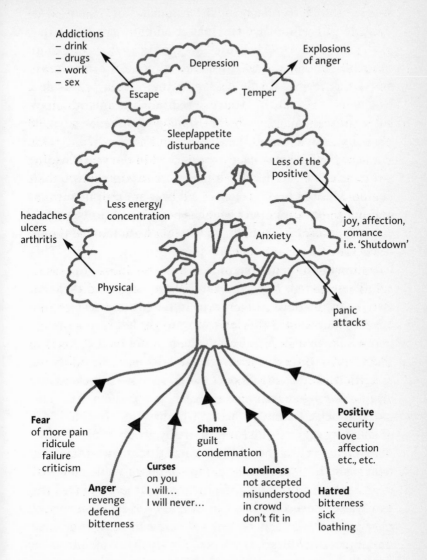

Figure 4

someone has hurt us, maybe intentionally. They said something to put us down. They may even have caused us real physical pain. Or, the hurt was unintended yet their thoughtlessness wounded us. Hatred creates a bitterness and a sick feeling inside us. We loathe certain people and whenever we meet them we are reminded of the hurt they have caused. When we hear them mentioned, the pain flicks into our mind.

Many people may have hurt us in our lives and if we are not careful we can develop a pattern of hating each one. A person who has been attacked and beaten up finds it difficult not to hate. A person who has been raped finds it difficult not to feel bitter. A person who has been let down finds it very difficult not to hold it against the culprit. This hatred is in our root system.

Then there is *fear*. For example, we may know that certain people will probably hurt us in the future because they have already hurt us. "I don't want to get hurt again. I fear being in such a situation when I am going to get hurt like that again." Or we can fear ridicule, failure, being put down or criticized. Out of this part of the root system can come all sorts of associated feelings such as irrational fear and panic attacks. I knew someone who had an irrational fear of standing up to speak in front of any group of people. Not many of us relish the idea of doing that anyway, but this fear was so intense that the person felt paralysed and found it difficult to continue with a degree course. In prayer the fear was discovered to have originated through episodes of ridicule at senior school. The ridicule had been expressed not only by fellow students but also by the teacher. It had hurt deeply and was still part of that person's make-up.

Next there are *curses*. Whereas in Step 4 we repented of the curses we have placed on ourselves and the sin we have fallen into as a reaction to curses placed on us, here in Step

4$^{1}/_{2}$ we deal with the hurt caused by those cursing us. I recall someone who was told continually by their father, "You'll never be any good. You'll never be any use in this life. You'll always fail. Just look at you – you'll never be any good." In that short speech there are so many curses. Not only did the curses have power in themselves to affect the person's life, but that person also appropriated them to themselves. They became part of their belief system. They thought of themselves as useless and no good.

It's not always about what we have or haven't done, either. I recall a young woman who was quite unaware of her beauty. In fact, she was discontented, "knowing" she was ugly. She had been told this so many times by her mother that she had come to believe it and it was now part of her root system.

Then there is *shame*. Some of those who work with people who have addictive problems say that shame has the most debilitating effect in people's lives. Condemnation and guilt are part of shame. It is what Adam and Eve felt, and it caused them to change their attitude and their actions and to hide from God himself. They felt shame, they covered themselves up and inwardly knew they had sinned. Sometimes, when a person cannot meet our eyes or when they walk around with their head bowed, we know that shame is not far away. When a person has low self-esteem the root can often be shame.

Yet this shame is not always of the person's own making. It is sometimes put upon them by the actions or words of others. For example, it is common for a child who has been abused to believe in some way or other that they were responsible, that it is their fault. In fact, sometimes the perpetrators of the evil put that sense of responsibility upon the child, that it must become "their secret". This secret is the very foundation of their feelings of shame.

Abuse is such a complex issue, especially when it is done by those who are trusted by the victim. I recall praying with a young man who so wanted his father to love him that he even allowed him to abuse him sexually in order to seek that love. Yet he felt shame from that time on due to that abuse. It affected his whole being. There was shame both from the abuse itself and from his compliance with his father's actions.

Now look at *loneliness*. Being lonely is a strange thing. You can stand in the middle of a crowded room and be lonely. You can be on your own and not be lonely. The truth is that loneliness is to be found within us rather than in situations. Such feelings may come from not being accepted by those around us. Maybe they come from being misunderstood or from being left out of the crowd. Children can be very cruel to each other and whether you are in the "in crowd" or not is very important. If you are a girl, it is necessary to have a "best friend". For boys, maybe it is being part of a gang. The traditional way of picking sides for any game in the playground has the potential for lasting hurt! To be the last one or two "picked" for the respective sides is usually devastating. This loneliness takes root and needs dealing with.

We must look again also at *anger*. Even though we show in Step 4 the need to repent of our anger, sometimes it is only in Step 4½ that the root of this anger is seen clearly. It is to do with revenge and it is also to do with defending ourselves. ("I am going to get them before they get me and hurt me again.") People often live with a bitterness deep inside. Many suns have gone down and anger has remained. I was talking to someone recently who said they never felt angry with anyone. It was true they didn't, but they had tried to commit suicide on three occasions. Why? Because they were so angry with themselves. Actually it was like a perverted reaction because when they began to look deeply into their past they were so angry with the people who had hurt them that they had buried that anger and it was pulsing away all the time within them. Yes, they knew they didn't feel right but it took work to uncover the anger.

These hurts in our root system unsurprisingly have an effect on our outward life. This is represented by the tree trunk and branches in the illustration. It is not always easy to see how one particular area of hurt has specific outward effects. But if we look across our lives and see different aspects of our behaviour that are questionable, the Holy Spirit will lead us to particular roots that need to be addressed.

Also we may, as Christians, have tried to cover hurt up and indeed on the surface even sought to forgive the person against whom we are angry. But that forgiveness may not reach our root system. Step 4^1/$_2$ makes sure it does.

Visible effects in our lives

It's time to look at the fruit of the tree (Figure 4). But beware. The reason we have problems in a particular area may not have anything to do with the root system at all. For instance, problems in our *sleep patterns or diet* may be to do with a chemical imbalance. We may not be able to sleep eight hours a night because, in fact, God only wants us to have six hours of sleep and to get up rather early in the morning to be with him! I have heard of someone who always had disturbed sleep following the drinking of red wine. What was the obvious solution? Well, not to drink red wine in an evening, just as some people do not drink coffee near to bedtime. But some of the problems may have a deeper cause.

Then there is a *loss of energy or concentration*. There may be a medical problem such as thyroid deficiency or a deeper reason.

Some people are continually *seeking escape* from their feelings or their situation. Many addictions stem from this cause. There is an escape through drink or drugs so that reality is left behind for a while. Don't let anyone tell you that taking heroin makes you feel bad. People need to know that initially taking heroin makes you feel good. You can leave your problems behind. You can leave your feelings behind. You can be on a "high". It is a way of escape and a powerful one. However, the escape does not last. You are left in a far worse place. Then there is the escape to work, to fill our time and give us a sense of fulfilment. Sex can be an escape too, as much of the "buzz" is in the anticipation and the imagining. These ways of escape take us away from the trauma in our inner being.

People also get *depressed*. That may be a clinical matter and they need help from a doctor. Often it is not, however, and drugs such as Valium or Prozac can be dangerous because they may immunize us from examining our hurt root system. We must be careful, though, not to advocate that people come off tablets that have been prescribed to them, without first consulting their doctor. However, as we look at our root system we may well find indicators for the depression. These can be frustration with unfulfilled ambition or thwarted plans. It is helpful to identify the cause of the unfulfilment or the plans that have been thwarted. If others were involved in some way then maybe they need to be forgiven.

Temper is the direct effect of anger in our lives. Some people are said to have a bad temper as though that is the real them. But is it? Although I treated anger separately when looking at our root system, sometimes it is linked to all manner of problems in our lives. We may well be angry because we are lonely, or because we are fearful, or because we hate someone. The question is whether the anger, the temper that actually becomes visible, is uncontrollable at times. Sometimes the explosion is completely out of proportion to the situation that provoked it. As seen in Step 1, temper can be an obvious sign that our life is unmanageable. Here we look at the cause and take this Step to find healing.

There is no doubt that some of the effects in our lives can be very *physical*. We may suffer from headaches, or we may have ulcers, or we may be prone to arthritis. Not all arthritis is due to something deep down, but on more than one occasion I have prayed with people and found that the physical ailment of arthritis has gone as a direct result of steps of forgiveness against the person that had hurt them.

Some people suffer from a continuous sense of *anxiety*. If you ask them why they feel anxious or worried, it is so hard for them to give an explanation. Why aren't they happy with their life? Why are they worried about what is going to happen next? Why does that person have a panic attack so regularly that they do not really want to venture out much? Sometimes the answer is because they have a deep down fear that needs to be dealt with.

Finally, as we look at the effects of this root system in our lives, we must not neglect the *lack of the positive*. The easiest way to explain this is through listing what have been called the "top 10 intimacy needs of people".[1] We all need certain things to enable us to develop into secure and wholesome people. Yes, we can receive these from God but we also need to receive them from people around us. Ideally, parents should give them to their children as they grow up.

1. Acceptance – people accept us in spite of our faults.
2. Affection – someone touches or kisses us and this says, "I'm here for you." Some children go through life without that affection.

3. Appreciation – someone makes an effort to recognize things about us that are special.
4. Approval – we are caught doing something good! Parents are often good at catching their children doing something wrong or bad and need to change the emphasis.
5. Comfort – someone is there alongside us. We grow up knowing that, if we are in pain, upset or just need someone present, someone is there for us.
6. Encouragement – someone urges us towards a particular goal.
7. Attention – this says to us, "I am going to listen to you. I am going to be interested in you. I'm going to give you attention because you deserve it."
8. Respect – that is, someone says or implies that they value us, show the worth that we have from God.
9. Security – someone is there to protect us and care for us. Once that would have been our parents. But there always needs to be people around us to defend us or to hold a hand when we are scared.
10. Support – we all need someone to say, "I will help you carry your load."

We need these things as we grow up and as we go through life's various situations, good and difficult. As we do Step 4^1/$_2$ we may need to list some of the people who should have provided some of these aspects of intimacy for us but did not. Then we can move to forgive them.

This is more difficult than listing specific hurts that arise because something has been done to us. This is a list of omissions, yet is just as important. We need to look at what we have missed in our life and then deal with it. Sometimes we can put specific people's names next to the omission. We can put actual events down. Sometimes these are cumulative, long term, or chronic. It isn't that we were not given the affection we wanted or needed at one particular time; it was lacking over a long period of time. Or there may be a particular event where you thought you were very close to someone but that love was not reciprocated. Or perhaps, instead of being accepted and loved by your parents, even with your faults, they seemed to cut you off at that point even though you were sorry for what you had done.

Let the healing flow

The effect of such hurts can be very powerful, so let us be clear what will happen when we look seriously at them in this Step 4^1/$_2$. God wants to cut off each negative root in our life, whether of shame, anger, loneliness or whatever. Before we pray for it, we need to do some specific action to enable the healing to flow.

We need to ask God for bravery and power so that we can go back with the Holy Spirit and look at the very hurt that has caused us pain. We look at our past lives and at those who have hurt us. We are to make a list of all who have hurt us in the past and put against each name all the events that we can remember that caused us specific hurt. These may be particular actions or they may be acts of omission.

We also need to ask God to show us the feelings we experienced at that time of hurt. This is no superficial thing. This is not about saying quickly that we forgive that person who has hurt us. It is getting down to the reality of what actually happened to us and how we felt about them. We get in touch with our feelings of hurt, but also face up to the sin that we committed by our reaction, such as hatred, anger or cursing. We need God's help to do this and we ask the Holy Spirit to reveal what we need to see about these events. We are not digging for things that are not there. It is the Holy Spirit's responsibility to bring to the surface whatever needs to be dealt with.

Having repented of our sins in how we have reacted to hurt, then we can also ask God to fill us with his love to enable us to forgive the person who hurt us. Some people have found it helpful to imagine holding that person in their cupped hands. They work towards the point when they are able to give that person to the Lord rather than try to crush them and hurt them. This may not be an instant process. If a person has been deeply hurt, then it takes some time to reach that point of forgiving the offender.

The best practical way to do this Step 4¹/2 is first to make a list of hurts under a person's name. It may be possible for us to take all the necessary steps on our own so that we repent of our sins of reaction and do, from our hearts, forgive the person who has done the hurt. But for most of us it is necessary to meet with someone else and pray this through with them. Indeed, my suggestion is that we should all seek out not only one person but two people together to pray with us about these hurts. God so often speaks to those whom we are praying with. They will be vehicles through whom God's healing comes and they will be able to assure us of God's forgiveness and perhaps also to encourage us concerning his purposes for the future, maybe as to how our habits will need to change now that the root has been cut off.

Step 4¹/2 is so important. However, we must see why it comes after Step 4. It has been my experience that many people have found it so much easier to forgive those who have hurt them because they have already repented of so much in their lives. It is as though God has used our repentance to soften us up to experience his love and forgiveness for those who have hurt us.

Here is a woman's testimony to just this experience:

When I look back on my life since becoming a Christian, I equate it with having been put in a washing machine! For the first four years or so I was on a "delicate wash", gently coming to know Jesus and to see myself through God's eyes. Then I came to St John's and God pressed the "fast spin" button! I began to do the 12 Steps and it has been an amazing time. Often incredibly painful, yet so filled with God's presence and leading that the only way was forward.

I've realized that much of my life has been formed around the damage I suffered after having an abortion at 15 years old. The pain, shame and guilt I carried from that kept me away from church, despite believing in God, until I was 30 years old with young children whom I wanted to raise in a Christian fellowship. Working through the Steps meant I could then ask God to forgive me, and the Steps have continued that work of forgiveness and restoration that I so needed to receive. I also found the strength to lovingly confront my parents and explain that their solution to "the problem" had left me devastated for many years. I was able to say sorry for putting them in that situation and to tell them that I forgave them their part.

I believe I am now becoming the person God created me to be.

Now share your list from Step 4¹/₂ by way of Step 5. However, do make sure you have *already* completed the process of sharing your list from Step 4.

A prayer:
Thank you, Lord God, that you know all about the hurts that I have experienced in my life. Thank you that none of them are hidden from you and thank you that you have the power not only to bring them to the surface but also to rid them of their crippling

power. Lord God, help me to take responsibility for the sins of reaction I have committed. Help me to look in detail at the situations and at the people that have hurt me. Help me to receive your power and love to forgive them. Lord, may I see these roots cut off in my life and may I know your fruit growing in my life. Build new habits into me, I pray, so that I put into practice the freedom you are now to give me. Through our Lord Jesus Christ. Amen.

Taking the 4¹/₂th Step

Step 4¹/₂. We recognize the hurt in our lives. We forgive those who have caused it and we ask for it to be healed.

Step 4¹/₂ calls us to deal with the hurts in our life. Look again at these injunctions from Ephesians 4 and 5: "Put off your old self... be made new in the attitude of your minds... do not let the sun go down while you are still angry... do not give the devil a foothold... get rid of all bitterness, rage and anger." Some of these wrong attitudes and actions flow directly from hurt that had been done to us in our lives. We take this Step 4¹/₂ to receive healing of our hurts.

1. Study again the illustration (Figure 4) on Page 71. Quickly identify any of the following negatives in your "root system": hatred, fear, curses, shame, loneliness, anger.

2. Again looking at the illustration (Figure 4), quickly identify any of the fruit of the tree present in your life: problems in sleep patterns and diet; loss of energy and/or concentration; seeking escape; depression; temper; physical symptoms; anxiety; addictions.

3. Look through the list of the "10 intimacy needs" found on pages 77–78. Going back even to your childhood, identify which of these you have lacked in your lifetime.

4. Make a list of all the times in your life that you can remember where you have been hurt. It may be easier to do this by listing hurts under a particular relationship: your mother, or your father, or teachers, or friends, or work colleagues, etc., etc. For each one try to do this chronologically, starting with the earliest event. Write out the detail as well.

5. Having made the above list, go through it again and add in your reaction to the hurt, identifying your feelings and what you did.

6. Now ask God who you should share this list with. Probably it is the person you shared the Step 4 list with. Preferably, though, as prayer ministry is involved, there should be two people.

7. It is vital that this list is shared by way of Step 5 *after* the sharing of your list from Step 4.

Step **5** *We admit to God, to ourselves and to another human being the exact nature of our wrongs*

To God *"As surely as I live," says the Lord, "every knee will bow before me; every tongue will confess to God."*
    Romans 14:11

To ourselves *This is the message we have heard from him and declare to you: God is light; in him there is no darkness at all. If we claim to have fellowship with him yet walk in the darkness, we lie and do not live by the truth. But if we walk in the light, as he is in the light, we have fellowship with one another, and the blood of Jesus, his Son, purifies us from all sin.*

If we claim to be without sin, we deceive ourselves and the truth is not in us. If we confess our sins, he is faithful and just and will forgive us our sins and purify us from all unrighteousness. If we claim we have not sinned, we make him out to be a liar and his word has no place in our lives.

My dear children, I write this to you so that you will not sin. But if anybody does sin, we have one who speaks to the Father in our defence – Jesus Christ, the Righteous One. He is the atoning sacrifice for our sins, and not only for ours but also for the sins of the whole world.
    1 John 1:5–2:2

To another human being *Therefore confess your sins to each other and pray for each other so that you may be healed. The prayer of a righteous man is powerful and effective.*
James 5:16

It is probably not so much the confessing of our sins to God, or indeed to ourselves, that causes us the most fear and trepidation. It is the idea of confessing them, in detail, to another human being. Yet this is what Step 5 is all about. The initiators of the 12 Step Programme soon became aware that the back of addiction was often broken in the confession of sins to one another. Of course, they knew it was necessary to confess sins to God and it was also very necessary to admit our sins to ourselves to take away any façade, pretence or act from our lives. Yet until they confessed to another human being, people would often stay trapped.

The same has been true in our experience at St John's. This coming clean, admitting our sins to another person, is the most difficult thing to do. But it is the step of release and freedom that some had not even dreamt was possible.

Confession to God

However, we still need to begin with the necessity of confessing to God. By now, we should have a list written in response to Step 4 detailing the extent of our sinfulness of the past. If we have done this properly it will not just be a list of general headings but will include details of specific actions taken, thoughts dwelt on or words said. For example, we will not just have stated we have a problem with anger but will have detailed when that anger has been shown by us, when it has erupted and when other people have felt the force of our actions driven by this anger. If we stated that we have a problem with sex, we will have gone on to say that it relates, for instance, to looking at pornography. But then it also details what pornography has been looked at, when and in what circumstances. In other words, there are none of the secrets that can be kept through a "general confession".

In Romans 14:11 Paul quotes Isaiah 45:23 and states how every tongue will confess to God. The context for Paul is explained in verse 12, "So then, each of us will give an account of himself to God." The Bible teaches that we all have to give an account to God for our lives and indeed we all have to appear before God's judgement seat (2 Corinthians 5:10). In Revelation we read of how our actions will be noted, and there will be a record of our deeds (Revelation 14:13). We therefore need to take very seriously our confession to God.

Of course, I am aware that the Christian Gospel is that Jesus has taken the punishment for our sin and removed the penalty of eternal death from us through his death on the cross. I know he is our substitute in punishment. I know that our sins are wiped away. They are removed "as far as the east is from the west" (Psalm 103:12). However, I am also aware that the true personal, emotional release comes after specific confession to God of all our sins. Then the sense of shame is removed; the feeling of guilt and condemnation is dissolved and wiped away.

Therefore, as we bring our lists from Steps 4 and 4¹/₂ to this current Step 5, we are ready to confess to God the "exact nature of our wrongs". He is waiting for us to do this.

Confession to ourselves

The problem, then, is that we find it easy to lie to ourselves. How many of us really approach a time of confession in church with a heartfelt desperation for forgiveness? If we are honest, we usually say any words of confession with the contempt of familiarity or a certain amount of apathy. Were we really *that* bad last week? Our minds may even go blank and we can't think of one thing we have done wrong. We have got used to living on a shallow level of awareness of our sin.

John addresses this in his first letter. His language is challenging and penetrating. "If we claim to be without sin, we deceive ourselves and the truth is not in us" (1 John 1:8). Let us not forget that Jesus described himself as the truth. Could this really mean that Jesus himself can find no place in us because of our self-deception? Previously John had said, "If we claim to have fellowship with him yet walk in the darkness, we lie and do not live by the truth" (1 John 1:6). We come back to the accusation often made against Christians, that we are hypocrites! Jesus often accused the religious leaders of it. The dictionary definition of hypocrisy is "concealment of true character".

The trouble is that often we do not recognize this hypocrisy in ourselves, and have got so used to ways of self-deception that it comes as a shock to realize that actually we do sin regularly and often, and so destroy our fellowship with Jesus. Nevertheless, as we come to Step 5 we should already have seen some of this deception broken down and the denial of our responsibility challenged. It is ready to be swept away now in confession.

John points out the tremendous benefits of confession. He states that God "is faithful and just and will forgive us our sins and purify us from all unrighteousness" (1 John 1:9). Thank God that he is faithful to us even though we so often prove faithless and let him down. Praise God that he is just and he knows the truth of our situation and can forgive us because that sin is placed upon Jesus dying for us on the cross.

Not only does John talk about this forgiveness but he

gives a graphic picture of Jesus speaking to the Father on our behalf. He then shows us another picture of Jesus being sacrificed there on the cross in our place. It is personal for us; it is also personal for everyone in the world (1 John 2:1–2).

Confession to another human being

In my years of being a minister I have spoken to so many people who testify to the fact that they never knew they were forgiven for a particular sin until they openly confessed it to another human being. I can remember a man who confessed a sexual sin he had committed 15 years previously. Over and over he had confessed it to God, and he had no self-deception either. Yet he never really believed he was forgiven. He always believed this sin was between him and his Father in heaven. In theory he knew Jesus had died for that sin on the cross but he just never felt it was taken care of. However, when he did confess it to God in my presence and I was able to pray prayers of absolution and forgiveness for him, the weight lifted off his whole being. His mind became clear and he knew he was accepted by God, forgiven by God, cleansed by God and restored by God.

No wonder James tells his readers to "confess your sins to each other and pray for each other so that you may be healed" (James 5:16). Roman Catholics still provide the opportunity for people to make their confession to God in the presence of the priest. I have talked to many who have found this practice a great release. However, for some the Catholic practice has been devalued and undermined. The confession has taken on the admitting of sins in a very generalized way without true repentance and the decision to turn away from that sin. Even though the confession has been made, the intention is still there to do the same sins next week!

This is not to say that the Catholic priesthood condones such action, but it is a common practice nonetheless. Also, the system of penance may devalue this act of confession. Although to have to say three "Hail Marys" or two "Our Fathers" may be designed to concentrate the sinner's mind onto the things of God, this does not follow the biblical teaching about repentance, forgiveness and changed lives.

We have lost the value of confession. Luther said, "Confession is useful, even necessary. I would not have it abolished. Indeed I rejoice that it exists in the church of Christ because it is a cure without equal for distressed consciences. For when we have laid bare our conscience to a brother and privately made known to him the evil that lurks within, we receive from our brother's lips the word of comfort spoken by God himself. And if we accept this in faith we find peace in the mercy of God speaking to us through our brother."[1]

The word "confess" is used in the Bible not only for the confession of "sins" but also for the confession of "faith". We see that the speaking out of faith is important for Christians. Romans 10:9 says, "If you confess with your mouth, 'Jesus is Lord', and believe in your heart that God raised him from the dead, you will be saved." He goes on to say, "For it is with your heart that you believe and are justified, and it is with your mouth that you confess and are saved." He reiterates in verse 13, "Everyone who calls on the name of the Lord will be saved."

The same can be seen in Philippians 2:11, "And every tongue confess that Jesus Christ is Lord to the glory of God the Father." It is still true that when people who believe in their hearts confess to those around them that Jesus is their Lord, they move to a different dimension in their Christian experience. Some people find it very hard to say to their family and friends that they have trusted in Jesus as their Lord and Saviour. But once they do, the conversion process is cemented and their faith becomes assured.

This confession to others is for many a hammer blow upon their sinful condition. It was dramatic in Ephesus when many new believers "came and openly confessed their evil deeds" (Acts 19:18). The practice of sorcery was confessed and acts of repentance included burning books of black magic.

Some have described Step 5 as being like a filter, just as a car needs an oil filter and an air filter to take out the impurities that would otherwise damage the engine. The open confession to another human being helps to filter out the impurities and dross that damage our lives.

Although Step 5 is born out of the biblical practice of confession, we are specifically speaking here of a major one-off event. It is the sharing of our lists, of our inventories, as written in Steps 4 and 4$^{1}/_{2}$, with another human being. Hopefully, in the future there will be no such long detailed list. This is a clear-out that is mould-breaking and life-changing. How then should Step 5 be done in practice?

Here are some practical pointers:

1. *Pick the person*
   For some people it seems natural to find a good friend to share this intimate confession with. For others it seems obvious that it should be a stranger. There are no hard and fast rules on this except that the person must be someone we trust. We are going to share intimate details and we need to know that they can keep a confidence and that if they are a friend then they can also cope with the revelations made to them. For many in St John's it has been someone in their cell group. Obviously it is helpful if the person also understands the Step programme. It's even better if that person has themselves

done Steps 4, $4^{1/2}$ and 5 in the past. The person also needs to be non-judgemental, so long as they will not trivialize what you are doing. It is unhelpful if they say to you, "You don't have to do this: God already has forgiven you." If that ever happens, you just need to thank them for their time and find someone else!

2. *Prepare the person (and you)*
   The person is being asked to witness us telling God what we have done wrong. This may involve listening to us as we tell God the details. It may instead be witnessing what we have written down to God by reading such a list. If we are speaking out, which is recommended, then it is helpful if the person does not interrupt continually. We are, however, giving them permission to give some feedback at the end. That feedback may include a challenge to give more detail than has already been revealed. The person you are sharing with must have some sensitivity and discernment here. If important detail has been concealed or repressed then this should be revealed. However, it is not necessary to go into more detail just because the person is curious!

3. *Procedure*
   (a) Although it may seem obvious, it is necessary to make an appointment to take Step 5. Give enough time for the appointment so there will be no interruptions (especially the telephone) and there will be no need to dash off at the end. Be aware at this stage that more than one appointment may be necessary.
   (b) When the meeting takes place it is helpful to go through Steps 1, 2 and 3 briefly at the beginning so that the firm basis of faith is there before the confession starts.

(c) Take your written lists with you. My advice is that a Step 5 relating to Step 4 (i.e. our catalogue of wrong-doings) is best done on a one-to-one basis with a person of the same sex. When you come to Step 4^1/$_2$ it is advisable to make this confession before two people, as God so often uses more than one person to minister to us in the healing of our hurts.

(d) Even while we are making confession it is necessary to listen to ourselves if we can. We may find ourselves justifying our actions or sinking into self-pity. We may even have more revelation of our situation while we are confessing. God sometimes gives us a different level of repentance as we realize it's not just the action that was wrong but also the motive behind it.

(e) Don't hold anything back! One of our leaders at St John's who did his Step 5 many years ago is always saying, "If you leave a Step 5 with any secrets, you have not truly done Step 5."

(f) Do listen to the feedback given. James 5:16 makes it clear that we should confess our sins to each other and pray for each other. God may well use that person to direct you and guide you further. Also, their prayer can be "powerful and effective".

What then does God do? He does all manner of things. There is no doubt he brings assurance of forgiveness. People sometimes experience this physically, like the lifting of a weight or a lightness of heart or an uncontrollable desire to laugh. It sometimes prompts people to cry. In addition, however, God will be cutting off the roots to the destructive feelings and behaviour in our lives. Such feelings do not always come at once. Indeed, Step 5 may not be completed in one sitting. But at all times God will be at work, cleansing us and freeing us. In addition, he will be touching particular areas of weakness in our life. If it has been low self-esteem, he will want to come and build our self-worth in the knowledge of our inheritance of his kingdom, that we are his sons and daughters. If it is loneliness, he will want to cut off that root and bring contentment in ourselves, whether or not we are in company. For some it may be plain freedom to enjoy ourselves more.

God then wants us to move on and build new habits in our lives. This takes us on to Steps 6 and 7. But for now the challenge is: will we get on with Step 4, Step 4¹/2 and Step 5? These steps are the crunch points of the programme. They are truly life-changing. Let me end this chapter with a testimony from a young mother about taking Step 5:

> All of my life I can remember there being fear. Fear of the dark, fear of rejection by others, fear of evil presences, being alone in the house and loneliness. The list goes on and on.
>
> Some nights I wouldn't be able to get out of bed to go to the toilet because of the fear of what I would find on the way or what was hiding by my bed. As I got older this reached the point where I would need to wake my husband up to pray for me because I couldn't pray myself. This would be after lying there for some time trying to pray to no effect.
>
> Over the last few years I had asked people to pray with me about these fears. Each time I felt a little more reassured but the fears were still there. I'd even been anointed with oil by one vicar because of bad dreams.
>
> Through talking to a friend who shared similar fears I realized for the first time that I could see them go completely. I was angry that they had trapped me, and felt a tremendous urge to be rid of them. I didn't want them controlling me any more.
>
> I asked two friends from church to pray. First I had to make a list of all the fears and times I had been afraid

through my whole life. I also wrote down everything connected to these fears and the people involved. These lists were then grouped under headings linking similar stuff. We then prayed through the lists at a number of meetings over a two-month period.

It has been different since then. For instance, in the middle of one night soon after I felt scared. The old feelings that used to be there were coming back, but what was so amazing was that they only lasted a moment. I prayed and asked God to forgive me for being afraid and to protect me, and it was fine. The fear lifted and I went back to sleep with no worries. I was able to stand and say the names of the two people who'd prayed for me as my witnesses.

Now I am free, completely. After those two months of praying I felt so light, like many burdens had been lifted. It wasn't easy during those times – when I began the prayer I had a particularly dark week – but by the end it was worth it. There was no power of fear left. No foothold. Nothing to hold me from believing God is in control.

A prayer:

Thank you, Lord God, that you know me so well. You know the fear that I have of sharing my innermost secrets with others. Yet I thank you for the release that I see can come from such confession. Lord, fill me with your power and your strength and such a knowledge of your love that I might take this step. May I know you are faithful and just. Thank you that I can confess my sins to you. Thank you that you are the truth and you want me to be true to you and to myself. Help me to confess my sins to myself. Then show me, Lord, the person to whom I should confess my sins. Do anoint them for this task and help me to be honest and open before them. Lord, come by your Spirit to help me. I pray this in Jesus Christ's name. Amen.

Taking the 5th Step

Step 5. We admit to God, to ourselves and to another human being the exact nature of our wrongs.

Step 5 is the practical Step of sharing the lists we have made under Step 4 and Step 4½. Although Step 5 talks of three admissions, namely admitting our sins to God, to ourselves, and to another human being, in fact all three can be done in one act at one time.

1. Pray again as to who God wants you to share your Step 4 list with. Beware, there might never be in our minds that "right" person to share these things with. Do trust God at this point and don't delay. Having made the list in Step 4 it is important to get on and share it.

2. Prepare the person so they know what you are coming to see them for, and make sure enough time is set aside (probably 1½ hours) and that the phone is off the hook and there are no other interruptions. Then follow the procedure detailed in this chapter (p. 91).

3. Pray again as to who should pray with you over the hurts as listed in Step 4½. Try to find two people to do this, preferably one of them being the same person with whom you shared your Step 4. Then follow the procedure detailed in this chapter (p. 91).

4. To clarify, Step 5 will come immediately after Step 4 and then Step 5 will again come after you have done Step 4½.

5. In your notebook it may be good to record the name and telephone number of the person you chose to hear your

Step 5 and the date you did it. Also, how you felt as you did it, and afterwards. It would also be good to note any new things that emerged as you were talking.

6. Keep your written Step 4 and any additional notes because they may be helpful when you take Steps 8 and 9.

We are entirely ready to have God remove all these defects of character

Therefore, I urge you, brothers, in view of God's mercy, to offer your bodies as living sacrifices, holy and pleasing to God – which is your spiritual worship. Do not conform any longer to the pattern of this world, but be transformed by the renewing of your mind. Then you will be able to test and approve what God's will is – his good, pleasing and perfect will.
   Romans 12:1–2

Alcoholics Anonymous literature includes a prayer known as "the serenity prayer" by Reinhold Niebuhr. It says, "God grant me the serenity to accept the things I cannot change, courage to change the things I can, and the wisdom to know the difference." There is some good wisdom in that, but we are not always ready to apply it to our hearts!

Someone recently faxed me a different serenity prayer and said this prayer much more fitted their mood. It read: "Grant me the serenity to accept the things I cannot change, the courage to change the things I cannot accept, and the wisdom to hide the bodies of those I had to kill today because they got on my nerves. And also, help me to be careful of the toes I step on today as they may be connected to the feet I may have to kiss tomorrow. Help me always to give 100% at work: 12% on Monday; 23% on

Tuesday; 40% on Wednesday; 20% on Thursday; 5% on Friday. And help me to remember... when I am having a bad day and it seems that people are trying to wind me up, it takes 42 muscles to frown, 28 to smile and only four to extend my arm and smack someone in the mouth!"

Sometimes we kid ourselves that we would be fine so long as we didn't have to meet other people. They are the problem because they provoke negative reactions in us. But our twelve steps are about acknowledging *our own* weaknesses, and indeed our own sins. By this time we should have a clear picture of how we do "fall short of the glory of God" (Romans 3:23). Now we are ready for God to remove our defects. But first, let us recap where we have got to, because many people are tempted to relax after taking the momentous Step 5.

Step 1 – we admitted we were powerless and our lives unmanageable, as we succumbed time and time again to the "sin disease". We took stock of how our lives, to some degree or other, were in a state of chaos.

Step 2 – we believed that God could restore us to sanity. God alone had the power to do something about our sin and could change our chaos into creative manageability.

Step 3 – we took the specific step of giving over our wills and our lives to God. You will remember we looked at the *one two three, one two three, one two three, one two three...* 12 Step waltz, and saw how we must press on to Steps 4 and 4$^1/_2$ and Step 5. Step 3 was a commitment to continue with the steps right the way through to 12.

Step 4 – we made a fearless and searching inventory of our moral lives. It was necessary to go into great detail about our past life and sin that we had committed and the hurt that we had caused. We needed to do this methodically, writing things down, going beyond the general to the specific.

Step $4^{1}/_{2}$ – only after we had acknowledged our own sin did we allow ourselves to look at the hurt that had been done to us. We therefore made a searching inventory of our hurts and sought God's help to forgive those who had caused them. We also looked at the consequences of this hurt in our lives to see how we had been damaged and also to see whether we needed not only to forgive but also to repent.

Step 5 – we admitted to God, ourselves and another human being the full extent of our wrongs. We saw what a difficult step this was, as most of us are not in the habit of making such confessions. Nevertheless, we saw what benefits this would have for us.

There is quite often a small delay in this process before moving on to Step 6. There are a number of reasons for this. One is that people often feel a sense of great relief having done Step 5 and naturally take a break. Secondly, people experience a tremendous sense of release as God ministers his healing to them. Sometimes they even experience euphoria when the guilt and shame is removed, and the hurt healed. Thirdly, people feel, wrongly, that now they have done Step 5 they can relax and forget the rest of the Steps.

Although Steps 1 to 5 are vital for lasting healing and change we must press on with Step 6 and the rest of the Steps. This is because God wants new habits to be taken up in our lives. He will have done the major work in breaking the bad habits of the past, but now he needs our attention and our co-operation to instil new habits into the various parts of our lives that were previously damaged.

However, before looking at Step 6 in detail it is necessary to give another warning. Experience has shown that some people, unlike those who want to delay, really cannot wait to get on with the steps and move too quickly onto Step 6 when they have not really done Steps 1 to 5 properly.

Although it may be attractive to ask God to remove all our defects of character as soon as possible, Step 6 (and Step 7) will only be effective if Steps 1 to 5 have been done seriously and thoroughly.

Step 6 says that "we are entirely ready to have God remove all these defects of character". When I first came across the Steps and read Step 6, I thought, "We all want to do that, don't we? We all want God to get rid of our defects of character." However, after a little thought I began to wonder whether in fact we do. In theory it sounds good, but when we actually see what it means to the way we live day to day, perhaps we are not "entirely ready".

So Step 6 asks us whether we are "entirely ready". Then Step 7 takes us to the specific point of asking God to remove all our shortcomings.

I find it helpful to think along the lines of "ready, steady, go" for Step 6 and Step 7. In Step 6 the question is, "are we ready?" Then, after we have looked in detail at it, we have a "steady" resolution to move on to Step 7. In other words, this is not just a passing whim but it is a heart-felt decision to be different and to ask God to change us. Then comes "go" as we take Step 7 and "humbly ask God to remove our shortcomings".

Ready

There are a few questions for us here. The first is, *"Do we really want to have all our defects of character removed?"* We may well be willing to change, to be different, but we may also be tempted to pray prayers like, "I'm willing to let you, God, come and change me so that I can live out my freedom in the future, but I do like to eat a lot of sweets, I do like a drink every now and then and I am aware that perhaps I can drink to excess sometimes. I do like to have those sexual fantasies now and again, because life's got to be a bit exciting. And I do like smoking, well perhaps I don't so much like it but I do find it so helpful to not feel stressed out. Then I'm sure it's OK to have self-righteous anger now and again. I have to admit that I do like passing bits of gossip here and there – anyway, what are we going to talk about if it's not about what's happened to all the people we know? Then, it was necessary to take those little financial shortcuts and I may have to do that again in the future. Then there are ways I sense I'm better than others at times – but then I am sure that's how you must feel too!"

If we are honest, most of us pray in such qualified ways. We have a catalogue of "small ways" in which we want to hang on to defects in our character. In fact, we do not see them as defects. Instead, they seem to be natural and normal, and really just "who we are". We cannot actually conceive of ourselves as being radically different from what we are now.

But in the nature of this step programme we cannot afford to be superficial in any way. We must look at all our character defects, however trivial they may seem to us, or however precious they may be to us. We may not even associate some character defects with the pain of the past. But we need to be reminded that God is not in the business of taking part of us and changing it and leaving it there. Ultimately he wants to transform the whole of us, to be more like his Son.

Another way of describing Step 6 is to see it as the step of decision-making for sanctification. We need to ask searching questions. Are we now going to commit ourselves to the road of sanctification? Are we saying to God that we now mean business in becoming holy? We know that we cannot make ourselves holy but we acknowledge that God can. He can change us but he will only do that with our permission. He wants us to be "entirely ready".

The process of justification has already taken place, as we have seen in Steps 1 to 5. We do not need to go back to look again at those sins that separated us from God's fulfilling presence. We now know that the way God looks at us is through the atoning sacrifice of Jesus. It is "just as if I'd" never sinned. He has justified us. Nevertheless, we do still now have to offer our lives to God so that he can help us to change. We need to change so that we don't once again accumulate a massive list to be dealt with in a subsequent Step 4. We are resolute with God, saying we want to be different and we want God to change us.

Having asked if we really want our defects removed, we now have to ask the second question, *"Are we entirely ready to give up control?"* Sometimes our desire for control is not so easy to see as one of the more obvious defects of character. If we have a propensity to steal, then we will realize quickly that that defect of character must now go. However, control is much more subtle. It is difficult to spot, even though it pervades many areas of our life. When we see a problem in our life or even a defect in our character, our natural inclination is to try and get it sorted ourselves. Maybe in the past we didn't really understand ourselves and our inclination to control, so we would try and control people and situations around us until we felt better. But when that self-realization came and we saw the problem to be mainly in ourselves, we finally took the step of handing over control of our lives to God.

Now we have come to the point of agreeing with God that we cannot manage our lives ourselves and need him to do so for us. We need to follow his prompting and guidance and let him change our character so that this defect is also removed. In other words, are we ready to live our remaining life under the Lordship of God? If we do, he can then work in us by his Spirit and we will begin to grow in the fruit of the

Spirit (Galatians 5:22–23) – including Spirit-led self-control as opposed to our previous wrong self-obsessed control.

From my experience, trying to remove defects of my character has been singularly frustrating and unfulfilling. It is as though giving my attention to one particular defect seems to free another one to become prominent. I was trying to deflate an airbed recently. As I pressed down on one part all the air in that part was removed and I could feel the floor. However, as I then pressed down another part the original section reinflated itself. It was only when I rolled up the airbed, not allowing any air to rush back in, that the whole process was completed successfully.

In practical terms, if I focus entirely on my problem of anger, I can become insensitive to the needs of people around me. All I am doing is trying to make sure my temper does not get the better of me. I am not actually thinking positively about other people's needs. Or, if I am trying to spend more time studying the Bible each day, I find that having started on Monday, by Friday I am doing well, and have doubled the time of study. However, on Friday I realise that I have hardly prayed since Tuesday! And I have completely neglected to sort out my money. Part of the answer seems to be to do some overtime. But doing more hours, I find I then have little time to talk to God or to study the Bible. Can all this really be right? Doesn't God have some other wisdom and power for us here?

I remember being very surprised quite early on in my Christian life when I heard someone preaching on the fruit of the Spirit from Galatians 5. The preacher stated how God wanted us to grow *all* the fruit of the Spirit and that it was really no good being full of kindness if we were so often impatient. Some of us may have had a head start in certain of the fruit of the Spirit but when God is in control of our lives he wants to form and ripen *all* those fruit. I believe the same principle applies to our defects of character. God does not want us to neglect one defect while spending all our time controlling another. He is in the business of involving himself in the whole of our lives and changing all our defects. Didn't C S Lewis talk about God as the Great Interferer? It is a process. It is a lifetime's work. It's for us to open ourselves up to the Lordship of God and for him to do the work in us.

The third question is, *"Do we want to be free?"* In John 5:1–15 Jesus asked the man at the pool, "Do you want to get well?" (verse 6). That is the only occasion we have recorded of Jesus asking someone whether they want to get well. The man did not readily answer the question with a yes or a no. Instead he explained why he was not able to get into the pool. "Sir, I have no one to help me into the pool when the water is stirred. While I am trying to get in, someone else goes down ahead of me." That implies he put the blame for his condition on others and was paralysed by self-pity. We would probably feel the same, having been an invalid for 38 years, our only hope being some miraculous healing through the stirring of water close by.

However, Jesus in his mercy immediately healed the man. He told him, "Get up! Pick up your mat and walk."

I believe we should ask ourselves the same question that Jesus asked the man, "Do you want to get well?" The answer should always be "Yes, of course." However, in the years that I have been a minister, it has become clear to me that for some people that answer is not true.

The man by the pool had a complete life-changing experience. After 38 years of being an invalid, now he was healed and whole. How was he going to make a living in the future? He had been a beggar, and had not worked. It would be interesting to know whether he immediately went out and got himself a job. Also, people would now have to relate to him differently. They could no longer relate to him as the invalid, because he wasn't. I wonder if he found it easy to think of himself as whole and not as an invalid? If he had had many years of complaining about not having anyone to lift him into the pool, and complaining about how other people got into it before him, how easy would he have found it not to complain about other things in the future? Or did his healing change him on a deeper level, removing this character defect?

Without being judgemental or making sweeping generalizations, there probably are people who have moulded their whole life around a disability, an illness or some defect of character, often with accompanying self-pity. Of course, many others just long to be free and healed and released. Nevertheless, the question has to be addressed.

If we have done Step 4 and Step 4½ thoroughly and have shared it with someone in Step 5, we are free – but now do we want the consequences of that freedom? Because we cannot now base our lives on the hurt that someone did to us many years ago, we have to move on and be different. We cannot live in the shadow of our sins any more. God has freed us from them and now we face the question of whether we are willing to allow him to give us new habits based upon that freedom. He has forgiven us our sins. Now we move on. He has healed our hurts. Now we move on. We have forgiven those people who hurt us so we are in a different relationship with them now. We cannot hang on to any bitterness or hatred. We have dealt with that and we now have to live in this new freedom.

I recall a mother who had the pain of seeing her young daughter crippled and finally die. For many years that mother could not get past the hurt and actually laid the blame at God's door. Those around her saw the bitterness eat away at her until finally by doing Steps 4 and 4½ she found release. The person she felt had hurt her was God, but in the end she repented of the anger she felt. She "forgave" God and went on to repent of having blamed him in the first place. It has been exciting to see her change over the years into someone who can now help others who have suffered terrible pain. Looking back, though, she can see how she did not really want to be healed early on. Amazingly, she can see that she wanted to stay in the pain and bitterness and hatred. She said she felt it was not only "who she was" but also "who she ought to be". In a way she felt she owed her bitterness to her daughter.

Steady

Are we now "entirely ready" to have God remove all these defects of character? In order for this decision to be life-changing it must not be made on the spur of the moment or on an emotional whim. It is to be considered, reflective and heartfelt. In Romans 12, Paul writes, "I urge you, brothers, in view of God's mercy, to offer your bodies as living sacrifices, holy and pleasing to God." Do not pass over the magnitude of what God has first done for us. Look at how God is so merciful to us. Sometimes we forget how much we deserve God's wrath, and yet he comes to us with his mercy. We are totally unlovable and yet God in his love sent Jesus to die for us. May that be the motivation for this offering of our bodies as living sacrifices.

To be realistic, though, that is not always the direction we come from. We still tend to be selfish in our outlook, even motivated to do these steps and thereby hand over ourselves to God because *we want* to get well, forgiven and healed – rather than because we wish him to be honoured. Therefore we must take a step back for a moment and reflect again upon God's love for us and what he has done for us already.

Then, we are to offer our bodies "as living sacrifices". Step 6 is about being ready to do that. The essence of a sacrifice is death, and yet Paul writes about living death. But the paradox is powerful. Someone has died for us and now we are going to live for God in the future. That is "spiritual worship". It is to give praise and glory to God. It is to give him the honour that's due to his name. It is to bring glory to God the Father. All these things are now to happen by the way we live. Is this how we really see it?

How are we to build a new set of habits into our lives? Paul's answer is that a process will happen, "the renewing of your mind". We are going to think differently from now on. We are going to see how the old programming has been deleted. We are going to live in the future knowing that the roots of hurt in our life are now cut off. God now wants to give his mind to us, the mind of Christ.

Then what are we going to do with our lives? How do we find out what to do in our life? The answer is that when we have taken this step, the offering of our life to God, and received the renewing of our mind, then guidance will be there for us. God will lead us into "his good, pleasing and perfect will" for our life.

Are we now ready to do Step 6, this step of preparation for Step 7? Are we "entirely ready to have God remove all these defects of character"? We must decide.

A prayer:
Dear Lord, I praise you and thank you that you do want to come into my life and do promise to change me, to make me like you, to restore me to your image. And I pray, Lord God, help me to want that. May I be entirely ready for you to remove all my defects. Help me to accept your mercy, your grace, and your love. May I want to live in the freedom you now offer me. Lord, come to me and be the Lord of my life, not only my wonderful Saviour.

Lead me into your good, pleasing and perfect will for my life. I ask this in Jesus' name. Amen.

Taking the 6th Step

Step 6. We are entirely ready to have God remove all these defects of character.

God doesn't want us to begin again to accumulate a new list of sins and hurts like those we made for Step 4 and Step 4½. He wants us to be transformed. This means new habits and a new lifestyle.

1. Are you entirely ready to take this Step? Have you finished your Step 4 and your Step 4½ and your Step 5? If not you cannot be entirely ready, so go back and complete these.

2. To see if you are "entirely ready", examine areas of your life to see which sins you "like" doing. Be honest to yourself and to God. Consider when you are most likely to take back control. Also reflect on your life to see which habits have their basis in past damage or sinfulness.

3. Read again Romans 12:1–2 and pray these verses to God as you now become "entirely ready" to give him your life and to have him "remove all your defects of character".

4. Write in your own words your statement that you are now *ready* for him to remove all your defects of character.

We humbly ask God to remove our shortcomings

Therefore, prepare your minds for action; be self-controlled; set your hope fully on the grace to be given you when Jesus Christ is revealed. As obedient children, do not conform to the evil desires you had when you lived in ignorance. But just as he who called you is holy, so be holy in all you do; for it is written: "Be holy, because I am holy."

Since you call on a Father who judges each man's work impartially, live your lives as strangers here in reverent fear. For you know that it was not with perishable things such as silver or gold that you were redeemed from the empty way of life handed down to you from your forefathers, but with the precious blood of Christ, a lamb without blemish or defect. He was chosen before the creation of the world, but was revealed in these last times for your sake. Through him you believed in God, who raised him from the dead and glorified him, and so your faith and hope are in God.

Now that you have purified yourselves by obeying the truth so that you have sincere love for your brothers, love one another deeply, from the heart. For you have been born again, not of perishable seed, but of imperishable, through the living and enduring word of God. For, "All men are like grass, and all their glory is like the flowers of the field; the grass withers and the flowers fall, but the word of the Lord stands for ever." And this is the word that was preached to you.

Therefore, rid yourselves of all malice and all deceit,

hypocrisy, envy, and slander of every kind. Like newborn babies,
crave pure spiritual milk, so that by it you may grow up in your
salvation, now that you have tasted that the Lord is good.

    1 Peter 1:13–2:3

Ready, steady... GO!

"We humbly ask God to remove our shortcomings." We
have decided we want God to do this. So how do we humbly
ask God to do it?

First of all, let us make sure we understand what
humbly means. Humility has rather a bad press. Charles
Dickens's Uriah Heep was "ever so humble" but boasted
that he still had "a little power". Dickens gives the impression that humility is to be equated with insincerity, a
façade, an act. We make out we are nothing special and
could be gainfully ignored yet behind the scenes are scheming and manipulative. Another false image of humility is of
a pathetic person just there to make up the numbers.

These are not the biblical meanings of humility. For
instance, Paul encourages us to "do nothing out of selfish
ambition or vain conceit, but in humility consider others
better than yourselves" (Philippians 2:3). The Gospels picture Jesus humbling himself and going to the cross for us.
He had every right to remain at the right hand of the
Father in heaven, but he came to earth to suffer a degrad-
ing death on a rubbish tip outside Jerusalem. Yet Jesus did
not get his self-worth from his actions or his position. He
was assured by his Father that he was loved and special
even before he had started his ministry: "You are my Son,
whom I love; with you I am well pleased" (Luke 3:22).

Therefore the key to humility is to see ourselves as we
really are. This requires two things of us. First, *we need to
know our place* in relationship to God. We are human beings,
he is God. We are not very wise, strong, or loving. We are

physically small in the great big scheme of things. However, God is omniscient, omnipotent, omnipresent and all-loving. His wisdom is infinite, and his power knows no bounds. He is the creator who made the universe. Humility knows its place as a creature; it does not try to make itself into a god.

Secondly, though, *we also need to know how God loves us*, accepts us and ultimately forgives us and promises to restore us. In *Body & Cell*[1] I wrote about the source of our significance. The two diagrams "The cycle of low self-esteem" (a) and "The cycle of high self-esteem" (b) (Figure 5) show that by conforming to the way of the world we try to achieve so much in order to feel satisfied and ultimately significant. We believe that this will enable us to be accepted by God. We are worth noticing. He will be pleased with us. However, that is the cycle of low self-esteem.

In the cycle of high self-esteem we start with first knowing that we are accepted by God. We are all special and we are all accepted and loved even before we have achieved anything. It is out of this acceptance that we obtain our significance. Christians are heirs to the kingdom. We are sons and daughters of the living God. That is our significance. That gives us a real impetus to keep going, to know God's lasting sustenance. Then we are well placed to achieve much for the Lord, and for his kingdom here on earth.

Humility is therefore knowing who we really are in relation to the almighty, loving God, and being aware that we are significant in his sight.

This is liberating. When we know who we really are, we no longer have to put on an act. At St John's Church there are many people who would admit to having been obsessed with themselves in the past yet never knowing who they really were. Note this paradox: when we are obsessed with ourselves we miss seeing who we really are. If we are self-

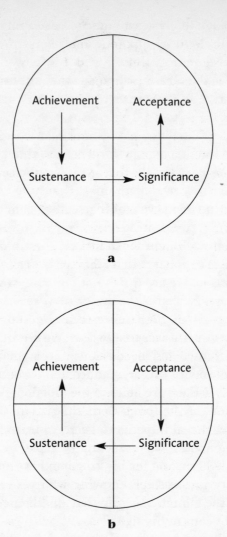

Figure 5

centred we are blind to our defects. It is so ingrained in us that we have a knee-jerk reaction at times that makes an attempt to cover up any defect.

I was once asked to sort out a relationship problem between two men in the church. They had argued and one came to ask me to sort out the other. He said the other man had been unreasonable in his demands and in his way of speaking to him. Amazingly, as I began to hear both sides of the argument and to talk things through with each of the men, I began to see that the first man, the one who had complained to me, was actually suffering from a sort of paranoia. He was not able to look honestly at himself and projected all the blame onto others around him. It took much time and patience to help him discover his own shortcoming.

Why are we sometimes like this? It may be that deep down we are afraid. We think we are unlovable. We may feel deep insecurity but only at this stage in the Steps does it come to the surface. Consequently in Step 7 we are taking a step of reality. We are saying to God that this is what we are really like. This is who we are. A sense of desperation can be good here. We are thoroughly fed up with what we are like and the way we act. Now, having received prayer and healing, we are desperate not to go back to living the way we had before and feeling bad about ourselves.

Therefore we humbly ask God to remove our shortcomings. This is a management issue: the business of our life needs to come under God's new management.

In the late 1990s Sir John Harvey-Jones, the former chairman of Imperial Chemical Industries (ICI), starred in a television series called *Troubleshooter*. In the programmes Sir John went to different companies that had problems and advised on their management. He went to one particular engineering firm that was struggling to manufacture and sell electrical components. Sir John gave various pieces of advice. However, it became obvious that the managing director was reluctant to take the necessary steps to sort out the main problems of the company. All the time he was looking at schemes to make different products that bore no resemblance to the original purpose of the firm. Sir John kept trying to steer him back to the real issues and the central problem. And so it is with us. Often we try to ignore the defects or shortcomings of our lives and spend time and energy on peripheral schemes to bring us success. Here in Step 7, though, we are going back to basics: who we are; what our defects are; how God wants to remove them; and how he wants to restore us to the image in which we were created.

Let us look at the management issues in more detail.

Going to the wall

This means the business has had it. It's over, finished. There is no prospect of success, prosperity and well-being if we carry on in the ways that we have lived to date. We are owning up to the unreality and pretence in our lives, and getting a grip on reality. Who are we really? What are we like? How does God see us?

Imagine the emotions that go through the owner of a business that "goes to the wall". Feelings of hopelessness and despair will only change if he sees a prospect of a way out. For us, the way out is a change of management. God's take-over of our life-business offers release, assurance, joy and purpose. This is no easy step to take, as pride so easily blocks the take-over bid. It is difficult to admit that we are wrong, or that we do not know the answer. The managing director needs to admit that he needs help. So do we. We need someone else to run "the company".

In our cell groups at St John's over the years it has been

exciting to see many people repent of this wrong pride and move on to reality. They have allowed the façade to be demolished. Amazingly, some people have even asked members of their cell group to be honest with them and tell them what they see of this façade in them. It has been liberating when someone has been told, for example, that although they were putting on the façade of being "a coper" it was obvious that this was not the reality, but that actually they were suffering from stress, anxiety and fear when they thought they were out of sight.

Let's be real, then. Let's give up the pretence and put aside the pride. Let us be willing to ask for God's new management.

The take-over

This new management for our lives is no makeover, it is nothing less than a take-over. We have already acknowledged that we will give control of our lives to God, as we took Step 6. Now we acknowledge what the take-over means.

The idea of "take-over" may seem negative. It conjures up images of the strong forcing the weak into submission, or the aggressive overpowering the vulnerable, or the large gobbling up the small. It may also suggest that the one taken over really did not want that to happen.

There is pain in take-over. But hopefully by this Step 7 we have brought the pain before God and he has come with his healing. It all depends on who is doing the take-over. This one is positive, not negative. It will not result in suffering but in fulfilment. This is no take-over for asset-stripping purposes. God is not going to take away all that is good and enjoyable in life, but rather will enhance our lives and fulfil all our potential.

How do you see your relationship with God? Think

about some possible images. Has he been a subsidiary? Has he been in partnership with you? Has he been in a merger with you?

If God were a *subsidiary*, we would be asking him to do what we want him to do based upon what we think will make our life better. If we see God as a *partner* we are assuming that we are equal with him. We will have some wisdom and he will have some wisdom. We will decide certain things and ask him to rubber stamp them, but we will let him decide other issues for us. The *merger* image is more subtle in that we see that he has another business but believe that his business would be enhanced by having our business join with him. In effect we are saying that we do certain things well that will complement or enhance the work of his kingdom.

But instead of any of these possibilities we need something much more radical. We are asking him to take over completely and be the new manager. God has to call the shots. He is to be more than just the manager. He is the owner. He is the sole shareholder and the only one to receive the profits. That is, the glory goes to him, the honour goes to his name. The benefits that come to us – the forgiveness, the removal of shame, the healing, the provision, the purpose – are all part of the new management deal and require continued submission to the new owner.

This take-over brings an amazing change. We will now reach our full potential. God knows what to do in order to achieve that. He will guide us into his good, pleasing and perfect will and God's image in us will start to be restored.

God wants us to see our life in relation to the kingdom. We are not to be concerned with fulfilling our own life, but we want to see God's glory evident in our world. We want to see his kingdom come in our locality. He wants us to be a functioning part of the church. He wants to equip us so that we can bring life to others. That may mean finding practical ways of helping others. It may mean taking part in projects that reach out into the community. It may mean teaching youngsters in the faith. There are so many possible areas of service. God can mobilize every member of the church and there is no doubt he has a role for each person to play.

God wants us to start dreaming dreams again. He wants us to have vision. I believe Martin Luther King heard from God when he said, "I have a dream." He had a vision of a time when the blacks and the whites in America would live in harmony and would have equal status. Walt Disney had a dream for Disney World. Someone once said that it was such a shame that Walt Disney never lived to see its completion on the site in Florida. However, the truth is he did "see it". That's why it came to be, because he had the dream, the vision.

God also wants us to deepen our relationship with him. He wants us to find out all that we can about him. We can read the Bible. We can study it. We can buy notes and books and versions of the Bible that help us to understand it. We can spend time talking to him. We can listen to him. We can worship him. We can listen to and follow the example set by older and wiser Christians. As we continue to experience his love and his peace in our lives and his healing, his purpose for our particular life will become evident. He then also equips us by his Spirit to fulfil that purpose.

Finally, as we look at the take-over, let us remember that power and authority are then to come to us in this new way of life. Matthew 7:29 says that people saw that Jesus was different and that he spoke with authority. That is what God also wants for us. He wants his power to be recognized in us so that people around us, in our network of relationships, become aware that we too are different, that

God is in our lives. We humbly ask God to come and complete the take-over.

A new business in the same building

Taking Step 7 is very simple. It is no more complicated than praying a prayer that asks God to remove our shortcomings. However, it is helpful if the prayer can be specific about them.

Having got to Step 7, we are well aware of the shortcomings in our lives. We therefore name them before God and ask him to remove them. If we take impatience as an example of one of our shortcomings, then we ask God to remove it from us. Then what does he do? My experience is that he often answers that prayer by bringing along numerous situations that frustrate us and provoke us. But then in those situations he promises patience. It is there for us to claim from him and now he gives us some training in recognizing situations that will require it. We often have the wrong view of how God works in situations like this. We think he will remove the temptation to be frustrated and impatient. Rather, he takes us through similar situations and trains us to respond in a new way.

Whatever our defects, as we take Step 7 and ask him to remove those shortcomings, God trains us in new habits of our new life. For instance, if we have a problem with sex and pornography, there is no way that he will protect us so that we never see any provocative advertisement, photograph or top-shelf magazine. Rather, he promises the strength to look elsewhere, or to walk out of the shop, or to go to bed instead of watching late-night television. But we do need to invite him into the situation and ask him to train us. Then we will see the old habit got rid of.

In Luke 11 Jesus told a story of a man who had a demon removed. The demon then went off and wandered around looking for a place to rest. Not finding anywhere, it went back to the same home and found that it was all swept clean. That demon, though, took back with it seven other demons. They got in because nothing had replaced that which had been driven out. It was empty, void. If we are going to get rid of the old stock of our lives we have to start creating some new "products", in God's way. The Bible calls them "the fruit of the Spirit" (Galatians 5:22–23).

Step 7 is about acknowledging that our lives have "gone to the wall" and now asking for the take-over. He is now to be the Lord for the present and future. We now humbly ask God to remove all our shortcomings.

A prayer:

Dear Lord, thank you that you want me to be entirely ready to have you remove all my defects of character, to have you take away all my shortcomings. Lord, I come before you today and pray for that reality, that humility, to know myself as you know me, as I really am. Come now and be my Lord and remove all these defects I now name before you. Give me the power to with-stand the temptations to act like I have habitually done in the past. Deepen my relationship with you, Lord, and show me your new way and give me the desire and strength to follow you. Through Jesus Christ our Lord. Amen.

Taking the 7th Step

Step 7. We humbly ask God to remove our shortcomings.

Having become ready to have God remove all our defects of character, we move on to actually asking God to do just that. Step 7 is a Step of action. Look again at 1 Peter 1:13–2:3. This passage is full of commands. Peter was in effect saying, "You've been forgiven, you've been healed, now get on and live out that freedom – be self-controlled – do not conform to the evil desires you had when you lived in ignorance – rid yourself of all malice and all deceit, hypocrisy, envy and slander of every kind – grow up."

1. In order to take this Step, firstly consider honestly before God whether you "know your place". We are to humbly ask God to remove our shortcomings, so we need to know that true humility in knowing our rightful place in our relationship with God. We need to know God's majesty and his holiness but also his tremendous love for us.

2. Now list before God your habitual shortcomings. Where do you keep on failing? What are your defects of character? Next to each one write what positive character traits could replace these defects, e.g. fear → courage. Now specifically ask God to remove these defects and shortcomings and give you new habits, new stock in your life.

3. Write down in your notebook the date you asked God to remove your shortcomings, and in the days to come you may like to also record times when you notice you behave differently – when it is evident that God has answered your prayer.

Step 8 We make a list of all persons we have harmed, and become willing to make amends to them all

Therefore, if you are offering your gift at the altar and there remember that your brother has something against you, leave your gift there in front of the altar. First go and be reconciled to your brother; then come and offer your gift.
   Matthew 5:23-24

Step 8 marks a change of focus. Steps 1 through to 7 have challenged us to look at ourselves and to come before God honestly, asking him to change us and to heal us. Step 8 looks outward instead of inward.

It's time to look outwards
We can measure our healing by how easy we find it to look out from ourselves. Are we aware of people around us and in particular those whom we have hurt and damaged in the past? We have spent most of our life looking after number one, ourselves, and not making a good job of it. We now realize that many of our problems are due to us. Now that we have taken action in Steps 1 to 7 to deal with that, we must go on to repair some of the damage we have caused

outside to others. If we do not have this outward focus, self-obsession may easily take over again.

Years ago, before we became a cell church, our congregation met in "fellowship groups" mid-week. However, these groups were primarily inward looking, concerned with the needs of members and praying through issues in their lives. People seemed to have more and more problems and issues to be prayed through as the weeks went by. A person with some problems would develop more problems as the original ones were prayed through.

When we made the transition to a cell group structure, we found a fundamental change took place. Because the cell group had an outward focus, namely to multiply within a couple of years, members were challenged to reach out with the Gospel to their network of friends, relatives and workmates. They also found that many people around them were hurting and that they could bring them hope. People who fully adopt this cell group agenda find that their problems are put in perspective and that God deals with them as they develop a heart for others around them.

Therefore in introducing Step 8 the same principle applies. Our focus is outward as we "make a list of all persons we have harmed, and become willing to make amends to them all". Yet, when doing this we also reap a personal benefit. God will continue to work on our defects and our shortcomings as we look outward.

Broken relationships

In Matthew 5:23–24, Jesus says that our worship of God is not acceptable if there is a broken relationship with someone close to us.

We do not always take Jesus' teaching here seriously. Many churches are riddled with broken relationships between individuals. It is a sad indictment on the church.

At times such broken relationships within the church are revealed in the press, but usually they are hidden and covered up.

We may feel bad about coming forward for communion if we have a broken relationship with another person in the congregation. We recall Paul's teaching in 1 Corinthians 11 about eating the bread and drinking from the cup of the Lord in an unworthy manner. We are supposed to examine ourselves at that time. The results of not doing so are shown by Paul to be serious, including illness and death. Jesus' teaching seems to go further than the communion service, however. I believe our gift as we come to the altar is not just the money we put in the collection plate, but our very act of worship as we come week by week to a church service or cell group (see Romans 12:1–2).

Obviously, if we are in a small cell group (say of nine or ten people) and there is a broken relationship between members, the resolution of that conflict soon becomes urgent and pressing. But we can lose that sense of urgency when we hide within a bigger group.

This scripture also points to two different scenarios. The first is where we know we have done something wrong to someone else, and therefore know that they have a right to feel aggrieved. Whether they do feel aggrieved or not is unimportant. We know we have done them wrong. We must put them on this list with a view to making amends.

Secondly, however, there are those who have something against us but we do not really believe we are at fault. Jesus does not make the distinction as to whether we have sinned against them or not. The phrase is: "Your brother has something against you." We must go to them to resolve this conflict.

The word used by Jesus for resolution of the conflict is "reconciliation". It reflects the reconciliation process that has already taken place between us and God. God reconciled us to himself through Christ (2 Corinthians 5:18) and that involved cost on Christ's part even though he was not at fault. He paid the penalty for our sin by dying for us on the cross. Paul goes on to say that we have this ministry of reconciliation. Primarily he means reconciling men and women to God, our priestly role. However, in conflict situations where we need to be reconciled with others, there may well be a cost, a price for us to pay. It will be a sign of our healing and new-found freedom if we can pay it willingly.

It goes against the grain

This step does not come easily to us. First, *we are likely to find ourselves justifying our actions*. We do not usually own up to our own shortcomings in relationships quickly. We have seen from the struggles we had in Steps 1 and 4 how it is an effort to own up to our defects, our sin. We may acknowledge that we have hurt someone else but we will quickly justify our actions. For instance, we say it was not surprising we flew off into a rage and hurt that person, because of what they said to us or what they did to us. We therefore excuse those cutting words we said back to them. We can see that to stop talking to them and ignoring them was a "good" method of letting them know how we felt.

Some of us have become so used to justifying our actions that it is out of our mouths before we know it. When someone says to us, "You are always late!" we immediately reply, "Always late? What are you on about? I was there on time last Wednesday and the Wednesday before." We have conveniently forgotten that we were late on Friday night and Sunday lunch-time.

Secondly, *it is natural for us to bury the incident*. We may try to continue our relationship with that person as if the earlier incident had never happened. We may remember it and we may be aware that they remember it but we certainly do not talk about it. We try to get on with each other but on a slightly more superficial level. We don't want to cause waves. We would shy away from any confrontation. We may take steps to avoid them. Over the years it has been interesting to see what has happened at St John's when there have been broken relationships. We have two morning services and although members of our congregation are very regular at one service or the other, when there is a broken relationship someone may turn up at the different service so they don't have to meet the person they have fallen out with. These people do not thank me for my enquiry as to why they have suddenly turned up at the other service. But enquire I do!

Then we may try to be nice to the other person in an attempt to make amends for what has gone on before but still do not talk out the incident. This is not making amends because there is no acknowledgement of having sinned. There is no listening to the other person. There is no desire to hear from the other person what has happened in their feelings and thoughts during and following the incident.

It may be against our natural inclination to take this step of making amends, but it is of God. It can be exciting when people are honest with each other and say what they really feel, and listen to the other person as they do the same. One of the joys in seeing our cell groups flourish has been the willingness of group members to go through conflict periods over weeks and months. Although cell group members may feel at the outset that they like each other and can work with each other, often things happen that threaten that fellowship. One member will not like the attitude of another. One member will be hurt by another. One will be thoughtless. Someone will say something rather cutting and hurtful without thinking. We can bury these things or we can work through them. If we work through them, we can then come to understand each other better and be in closer partnership as we work together to see our lives change. This is the cutting edge of relationships that is so needed by Christians.

This is a step of freedom for those we have hurt but also a step of freedom for ourselves. As we look outward, we also find that we will benefit inwardly.

It's another list!

There really is no way round making another list. Some people are "list people" and others find it hard to get things down on paper. There are different ways of making a list. Some just sit down and let God lead them into writing down names of those they have a relationship with, and think through incidents whereby that other person may have been hurt. One man committed himself to Step 8 by spending 10 minutes each morning asking God to bring to his mind another person who had been hurt by him. He was slightly shocked and amazed to find that he was still going after a month!

Obviously, it's no surprise that those who live close to us and around us are on that list. We hurt people if we converse with or meet them regularly. This is no easy step and is a painful experience for many. However, as someone once said to me, "Embrace the pain. Pain is OK. It is a powerful sign that you are alive!" In fact, going through these steps has released some into pain temporarily! One lady whose early years were full of pain had shut down her life and anaesthetized herself to experience hardly any emotion for a 20-year period. This was caused by her damaged relationship with her father. Looking back now she would not describe that as "life". It was mere existence. When God started to work in her life and brought to the surface some of the memories of the past, she found that she experienced great pain and yet also great release and ultimately great joy.

It's the Step before Step 9!

Step 8 is the making of the list, whereas Step 9 is actually making amends. The making of the list, however, demonstrates our willingness to go through this whole process.

Step 8 is often seen as the acid test as to whether we have successfully undertaken Steps 4 and 4½. If we have listed all our shortcomings in the fearless and searching inventories and have dealt with the pain we have experienced from those who have hurt us, then we have a head start in beginning this list in Step 8. There was just no way that we would have been able to contemplate making amends with all the denial we had before completing Step 4, or with all the pain that was so crippling before we completed Step 4½. We therefore can start to experience how God has come into our lives with his forgiveness and assurance of salvation on the one hand, and his deep healing and restoration on the other. The wounds are cauterized and are no longer seeping.

Here we begin to demonstrate that we are OK. Now we want to address those vital loose ends that have been so damaging to those who have lived around us. We are saying to God, "OK God, I am now willing to make amends."

A prayer:
Heavenly Father, thank you that I have been able to be real with you and admit before you my sins and shortcomings. Help me now to take the next step of admitting my sins against those around me. Help me to be willing to make amends to them for my

behaviour. Lord God, fill me with your love and your compassion and give me sensitivity to those whom I have hurt. Help me to be specific as I list these people before you. Send your Spirit to me to guide me in this, Lord, I pray in Jesus' name. Amen.

Taking the 8th Step

Step 8. We make a list of all persons we have harmed, and become willing to make amends to them all.

Having spent much of our time in the previous Steps looking at ourselves, we are now called to look outward and start to take steps to heal and restore our relationships with others.

1. Are you in principle willing to make amends to people you have hurt? Spend a little time thinking over some of those with whom you have a relationship of one kind or another. Can you imagine going up to them or writing to them saying sorry and making amends? Ask God to help you.

2. Make another list! Jot down various people (1) who you have done something wrong to, or (2) who you know have something against you. Be honest with yourself and see whether you have falsely justified yourself in these relationships or have tried to bury hurtful incidents.

3. Again examine yourself to see if you are now willing to make amends to these people. Be honest – are there still any exceptions? Ask God to increase this willingness as you now move to Step 9.

Step 9 *We make direct amends to such people wherever possible, except when to do so would injure them or others*

Why do you look at the speck of sawdust in your brother's eye and pay no attention to the plank in your own eye? How can you say to your brother, "Let me take the speck out of your eye", when all the time there is a plank in your own eye? You hypocrite, first take the plank out of your own eye, and then you will see clearly to remove the speck from your brother's eye.

Matthew 7:3–5

The manual of Alcoholics Anonymous, known by many as *The Big Book*[1], says, "The alcoholic is like a tornado, roaring its way through the lives of others. Hearts are broken, sweet relationships are dead. Affections have been uprooted. Selfish and inconsiderate habits have kept the home in turmoil. We feel a man is unthinking when he says that is enough. He is like the farmer who came up out of his cyclone cellar to find his home ruined. To his wife he remarked, 'Don't see anything the matter here, Ma, ain't it grand the wind's stopped blowing?'"

We may not be addicted like the alcoholic, but many

people have a similar attitude to that of the farmer. We are so caught up in the excitement of our new-found freedom that we are insensitive to the devastation we have caused in the past. Step 9 makes sure we do not move on without doing something to heal broken relationships and correct situations of conflict.

Jesus gave his vivid illustration of the speck of wood in our brother's eye and the plank in our own in the context of judging. We can easily judge the deterioration of a relationship with another person as being due to their motives or feelings and their accompanying words and actions. Step 9 asks us to take a good look at the plank in our own eye first. We may come to the point where we need to help the other person remove the speck in their eye, but as Jesus says, we can only do that after we have dealt with ourselves and can "see clearly".

Thinking it through

Before we rush out to make amends with all those that we have hurt, in accordance with the list we have made in Step 8, let us pause for a moment. There are certain matters to think through first.

The first relates to *habitual* hurts we have caused. This particularly relates to those who know us well and who have been close to us in the past. These people may well need convincing that this time things really are different. We've probably said sorry many times before – only to return to our old ways.

It is possible to make apologies sound very cheap. "I'm really sorry and I want to get things right with you." They may well reply, "Well, that's fine for the 250th time!" This is the difference between being sorry and actually repenting. With repentance, our actions change. People close to us will be looking for a change in our lifestyle. Perhaps we need to delay making amends with those close to us until they can see by our actions that we really are different.

As we make amends, we need to be aware that there are some *consequential* matters that may cause us again to pause. In the Alpha course, Nicky Gumbel gives the illustration of a man who, when he was converted, wrote to the Inland Revenue with a cheque for £100 which he owed and he had been losing sleep over. At the bottom of the note to the Inland Revenue he wrote, "If I still can't sleep, I'll send you the rest." As we make amends we may also need to pay back a debt or, if we have stolen or embezzled something, or defrauded someone, to own up and be aware there may be painful consequences. Obviously, we need to think long and hard on such matters. I know of a certain person who has actually spent time in jail following admission of certain of his actions through doing the 12 Steps.

We should not kid ourselves that the consequences of making amends will be to our liking. To make amends with someone we love does not always mean that the relationship will be fully restored. I know of a father who had consistently and persistently hurt his daughter. He had neglected her, let her down, sponged off her, and then ultimately disowned her. When he came to take this step of making amends, he found that he had so destroyed the relationship over the years that she was unable to forgive him and there was nothing he could do about it. Nevertheless, it was important that he made amends and his prayer is that in time the relationship will change, but he must take no steps to force it.

Thirdly, at times only *partial* disclosure is needed. It is not always wise to make full amends with someone. A graphic example is that of a man who had a sexual affair with a woman at his work. She too was married. Following Steps 8 and 9, how should he make amends in these circumstances? Would it be right for him to talk to the husband of the woman and make amends with him? Possibly it would be correct, if the husband knew of the affair. But if he did not know, should disclosure of it come from the man? That could have unforeseen and bitter consequences for the woman.

Taking Step 9 requires courage but also prudence. We are not always called upon to be bold and openly make amends. Sometimes we need advice. So we act with good judgement, careful timing and God's wisdom.

The danger is that we may know that we will benefit from making amends. We know we really need to talk to the other person so that we can get it off our chests and get the matter sorted out once and for all. It becomes an urgent need for us. We can then compound the original hurt by inflicting a new one on the person concerned. With good intentions, we are in fact moving back into the realm of selfishness not selflessness. Is it really helpful for the person to whom you are making amends to know all the sin you have committed in relation to them? Bear in mind that if we have truly confessed and repented (as in Step 5), God has already forgiven and forgotten our sin. So who are we to bring into the open what someone else was not aware of?

Who are we making amends to?

Obviously, for most of us there are different categories of people in our lives. First there is usually a group of *family and friends*. They know us quite well and when we are making our list we should beware of thinking that certain of these people do not matter. Take, for example, our children. We often find it difficult to say sorry to our children and truly make amends with them. Usually there are ongoing relationships, so we have to show that saying sorry is just the beginning. We are going to continue to make amends by our actions in the future. For instance, if as a father I have omitted to spend time with my son then it is one thing to say sorry to him but quite another to then spend time with him in the coming years to deepen our relationship together. Step 9 is never a quick one-off fix.

Secondly, our *"enemies"*. We have had something against them. We probably don't like them very much and we don't get on with them. This step of making amends does not mean we suddenly have to have warm feelings for them. We don't even have to like them. We don't have to work towards being buddies with them. Rather, God is calling us to go and see them, or talk to them, or write to them. The relationship with them needs to be sorted on our side. Obviously, to do this we first need God to change us, building on the steps we have already taken to get rid of resentments, hatred and anger. We should by now have forgiven them on a deep level if they have done things against us.

Thirdly, some of us may need to make amends to *ourselves*. This may come as a surprise. Yet some of us have given ourselves a very bad time over the years. We have put ourselves down, we have a low self-esteem, we have cursed ourselves, we have punished ourselves. Also, we have not allowed ourselves to have much fun. We have always felt guilty when we have had any fun. Some of us have gone so far as to try and punish ourselves after we had any fun!

In this whole Step process God has been peeling back the pretence in our lives to reveal our real self. We are now seeing that we must stop putting up those barriers and defences. We have already taken the step of allowing someone else as well as God and ourselves to know all about us, including all our sins and our hurts. We have allowed God to come in to change our lives and to remove our defects. It can be slightly scary to think what, if anything, is going to be left in us.

In fact we are going to be left with the real us, as God

created us. But we are not sure at this time what that looks like or if we'll like it. Nevertheless, in the process, making amends with ourselves allows God to build his image in us so much more quickly. I know of people who have specifically written to themselves to make amends. They have let themselves off. They have forgiven themselves and they have told themselves that with God's help they will be different to themselves in the future!

Finally, there are those *people who are beyond our reach.* Maybe they have moved away and we have lost touch with them. It is difficult to meet them face to face or even to write to them. Perhaps some have died since the hurt was done to them. Many people feel they have hurt in the past someone who has since died. It is still necessary to do something in relation to that person. This is difficult. We can't get in touch with them, and Christians know that seances are wrong and probably don't get in touch with the real person anyway. So what do we do?

Here are two suggestions. The first is that we talk to the person with whom we shared Step 5. We tell them how we want to make amends to the person who has died or who we have lost touch with. In effect, that person is standing in for the missing person. A second way is to write a letter to the missing person, put it in an envelope, write his or her Christian name on it, and burn it. (Don't post it as this may cause a headache for the post office, and you need to be aware that someone in the postal service will probably read it.) A number of people have told me how helpful it was to them. God had witnessed them making amends and the matter was laid to rest.

However, what we must *not* do is tell the relatives of the missing person all about our desire to make amends to them and go into details of the hurts done and the sins committed against that person. Invariably all that does is to stir up a can of worms and puts burdens on people. These are not their problems and they should not have to carry such burdens.

Do the results matter?

On one level it does not truly matter what people's reactions are when we make amends. They may tell us to push off or even worse! They may say it is no good trying to make amends after all this time. It will not be surprising for people still to be reacting to us out of the hurt that we caused them. We must leave them to their reaction. We must beware of trying to manipulate them into forgiving us. Sometimes we are so desperate to be forgiven that we will pester them and metaphorically "pin them up against the wall" until they do so. In living out our healing we should not need to have to be forgiven by them. Again, Step 9 proves to be an acid test of the forgiveness we have received from God and the healing we have experienced.

Also beware of trading amends. We say, "You did that to me and I will forgive you. Why don't you forgive me for what I have done?" This is not an excuse to look at how they may have hurt us in the past and would be irrelevant to our healing.

Step 9 is a step of action. We have gone through the process of deciding whether we are willing to make amends. We have also made the lists. Now we need to work out methodically how and when we are going to make amends. This may take us a little time and cannot be done in a day, or even a week. The temptation is to put it on the back burner so that we will deal with the matter only when a situation becomes acute. This is not what Step 9 is all about. It is being proactive and taking the trouble to make amends with those we have hurt in the past. There is no time like the present to start.

A prayer:

Thank you, Lord, that you do want freedom for me. Help me now to live out that freedom and to make amends to those around me. May I at all times have their blessing in mind. Change me from being selfish to selfless. May I have sensitivity, especially to those I have hurt, that they too can experience release and freedom as I am starting to. Finally, Lord, may my making amends not just be a matter of words but of actions, showing your love. Through Jesus Christ I pray. Amen.

Taking the 9th Step

Step 9: We make direct amends to such people wherever possible, except when to do so would injure them or others.

Those around us may have faults and may have hurt us in the past. Here, however, we are being honest before God and seeing where we must take the blame. As Jesus said, we are to look at the plank in our own eye before we look for the speck in our brother's eye.

1. Use the list you have compiled in Step 8 and make a plan as to how you are going to make amends. Against particular people's names jot down whether you are going to meet with them, or write to them, or telephone them, or just take all necessary action to make amends without actually being able to contact them.

2. Think this matter through thoroughly. Look again at what was said about habitual hurts, especially around those who know you well. Think of the consequences of making amends. List those people with whom you feel it would be harmful to do this.

3. Pray to God that you are not just doing this in order to obtain a "result" or to make yourself feel better. Talk

through with God the fact that you may not receive forgiveness from the person to whom you have sinned.

4. Go and make amends. Do not delay. Ask God for his
   power and his love so that you may take this action sen-
   sitively.

Step 10   *We continue to make personal inventories and when we are wrong promptly admit it*

And if I say to the wicked man, "You will surely die", but he then turns away from his sin and does what is just and right – if he gives back what he took in pledge for a loan, returns what he has stolen, follows the decrees that give life, and does no evil, he will surely live; he will not die. None of the sins he has committed will be remembered against him. He has done what is just and right; he will surely live.
    Ezekiel 33:14–16

In Ezekiel 33, the prophet was appointed by God as a watchman. He was responsible for pointing out the sins of the people of God. In stark terms he showed both the consequence of sin, "You will surely die" (verse 14) and also the salvation that was available, "[if] he then turns away from his sin and does what is just and right... he will not die... he will surely live" (verses 14–16).

Instead of having someone like Ezekiel to point out our sins, we have the Bible. Through his word God shows us his standards and rules for living. In the Steps programme we have developed a process based on these principles to help us live from day to day.

Step 10 is our commitment to going on living by these principles. In effect we are saying we will continue to do Steps 1, 2 and 3 (even daily if necessary) so that we do not accumulate such a catalogue of sins again.

Stop. Think. Pray

Every day we will find ourselves in situations that could provoke us to live as we did in the past. For instance, there will be situations where our anger could be provoked. Maybe we do not get our way at work. Maybe we are ignored by our friends who go off enjoying themselves without us. Maybe someone just does not listen to us or puts us down. We could easily react in our old ways, so how can we react in a right way instead? It is helpful to remember to stop, to think, and then to pray.

Stop (we know where we go wrong)

We now have a choice of how we act in any situation. We are no longer programmed as we were when we first did Step 1. We no longer have to react instinctively. We can hit the pause button. We can decide whether to be angry or not. Or at least we can catch ourselves becoming angry and make the decision not to let it boil over. It is the same with other triggers like fear or misguided zeal. For example, Peter in the garden of Gethsemane was volatile and under pressure. He pulled out his sword and he swung it before he thought about his action. From Jesus' response we can see that he did not want Peter to do this. Nor do we need to react in such "natural" ways.

We can now say to ourselves, "Hang on a minute – I'm powerless in this situation. I feel angry (or fearful or whatever) and I have the urge to lash out. But if I do, then the situation will really become unmanageable." The challenge for us in Step 10 is to apply this principle to our everyday life. It means we need to become much more aware of our feelings and our actions. It means acknowledging the healing that has taken place in us and claiming God's promises of power for living.

In 1 Corinthians 10:13 Paul says, "No temptation has seized you except what is common to man. And God is faithful; he will not let you be tempted beyond what you can bear. But when you are tempted, he will also provide a way out so that you can stand up under it." If we take the trouble to learn this verse there is a good chance that in a volatile situation God will remind us of it so that we can see the possible escape route laid before us. Of course it is not easy, but then Scripture does not say it is. It says we will be able to "stand up under it". In other words, the situation may remain as it is, with all the temptation to react wrongly; God may not remove it. But he will give us an inner strength, his escape route for us.

Think (we know who can help us)

In such a testing situation, we need to say, "Hang on a minute, I am going to do something I will regret later if I don't watch it. I feel powerless here and I'm not sure I can manage this situation. God, help me." We now believe that God can restore us to sanity even in a difficult situation that in the past would have easily provoked us to anger (Step 2).

We will receive a different perspective on the situation as soon as we invite God into it. It is the step of faith, acknowledging that although we may not be able to cope, God living in us by his Spirit can give us the power to do so. Instead of being blind to the situation and the destructive consequences, we start becoming aware of how God sees us and others in the situation.

Take King David as an example. He had a problem with

lust as he looked from his rooftop and saw Bathsheba. One thing led to another. Through David's detailed scheming, Bathsheba's husband Uriah was killed, David married her, and subsequently their child died. It would appear that King David was in denial of his sin for about a year before the prophet Nathan confronted him. The account in 2 Samuel 11 and 12 shows that David was suffering from a kind of blindness. He was not willing to acknowledge his sin or the consequences of it. However, the truth was that he was powerless over this sin and his life had become increasingly unmanageable. When Nathan rebuked David the scales, as it were, fell off and he clearly saw the extent of his depravity. He was then driven to God in the words of Psalm 51.

As we stop and think, I believe we will see clearly the extent of our sin and receive an increasing desire to call God in to change us and specifically to help us in particular temptations. Only God can help us and restore us to sanity. In Psalm 51 David says, "Surely I have been a sinner from birth, sinful from the time my mother conceived me. Surely you desire truth in the inner parts; you teach me wisdom in the utmost place" (verses 5–6). He sees himself as he really is. He then goes on to cry to God, "Cleanse me with hyssop and I shall be clean; wash me, and I shall be whiter than snow" (verse 7). Here he acknowledges that God can cleanse him. So he pleads for his future, "Create in me a pure heart, O God, and renew a steadfast spirit within me" (verse 10).

We know who can help us – God. He alone can renew a right spirit within us so that in any given situation we can start being proactive in right ways and not succumbing to the temptation to go down the old paths we were once used to.

Pray (we know the way forward)

In practical terms we must do more than just believe that God can restore us to sanity, we must also ask him to do so (Step 3). On a daily basis, and within each threatening situation, we can pray the prayer of Step 3 and hand over our will and our life to God. These are often called "arrow prayers". We say a prayer to God under our breath for him to help us deal with what we are facing. Of course, we have to hand over our will to him first. Perhaps in this given situation we want to throw a fit and lash out. But as we hand over our will to God we know that this is not how he wants us to act. Having stopped and thought, we now pray that his will be done in our lives.

Whatever we are doing, in whatever situation, we can put Step 10 into practice. We have talked about anger, fear and lust but the same principles could apply to very different situations and temptations. Maybe it is our tendency to gossip. Or it could be our powerlessness over greed, covetousness, or whatever. Paul reminded the Galatians of all sorts of sins in their past. The list is just as relevant to us today. "The acts of the sinful nature are obvious: sexual immorality, impurity and debauchery; idolatry and witchcraft; hatred, discord, jealousy, fits of rage, selfish ambition, dissensions, factions and envy; drunkenness, orgies, and the like. I warn you, as I did before, that those who live like this will not inherit the kingdom of God" (Galatians 5:19–21).

Many Christians in the past made a habit of speaking with God every morning and also in the evening before going to sleep. This is now often neglected. Step 10 fits such a practice, as it helps us to start each day with God. We can say to God in the morning, "I need your power; I need you to manage my life; you can restore me to sanity; you can take my life. Lead me."

Then in the evening before we sleep we can do a small inventory of what has happened during the day, acknowledge the sin that we have committed and ask for God's forgiveness. We can also talk to God about those people who have hurt us during the day, repent of our wrong reactions and ask God to help us to forgive them. It is well known that "a resentment harboured becomes a resentment hard to shift".

Obviously, if we have a daily routine that takes in this Step 10 there will be very little for us to include in a periodic inventory. Nevertheless, many people have found it of great value to look back on their lives every six months or so and see what has been happening.

That encourages them as they see how they have won some significant battles over past weaknesses and temptations to sin. They start becoming aware of new habits that are now part of their lives and routines that have become helpful. In the past they felt they would never change, but now they have a testimony about how they are changing. They can see specific events that previously would have provoked them to fall but have now become part of a chronicle of success.

But be warned. Some people who complete these Steps believe that each time they are tempted or each time a situation provokes them they will now have the power to be different and to win through. This is not always the case. It is helpful therefore to have a longer-term view of our lives and see that we have changed over a period of six months rather than become despondent because for a week or so we seem to have kept on failing. Sanctification is a notoriously slow process. In fact it will take us the rest of our lives! We must not get despondent.

For example, Gareth (we will call him) ran into difficulty at this point in the Steps. He had received spectacular healing as he undertook Steps 4 and 4$^{1}/_{2}$. He had been hurt very badly through sexual abuse in his youth. He started remembering details of this and received confirmation of them through talking to his mother. Then God did a dramatic healing in Gareth so that he could repent of his sins, especially the tremendous anger that was deep down inside him, and his feelings of unworthiness and sense of paranoia. He also was able to forgive the person who had abused him.

However, although Gareth had been changed in this significant way, he neglected to build new habits into his life. Although the root of the paranoia had been cut off, he subsequently began to dwell again on those feelings and neglected taking any inventory over his present actions. Soon it became clear that, although he had experienced a release initially, he did not want to give up the right to harbour resentment or paranoia.

Step 10 is there to help us build a new history. It allows us to translate past healing into present freedom. It enables us to move on from having the guilt and shame removed to a readiness to admit our sins today.

Let me end with another example. Suzanne (we shall call her) came from a broken home. She did not get on with her stepfather and experienced serious neglect between the ages of 9 and 13. During her teenage years she rebelled and gradually became dependent on drugs. She also became a prostitute. As she began to work through the Steps of this programme an amazing transformation took place in Suzanne's life.

She found she was able to catalogue her sins in such great detail in Step 4 that it nearly became a book! Also, her emotions were opened up so that she could see clearly what her feelings had been in her early years. She worked through these and came to that point of forgiving those who had hurt her and subsequently repenting of the way she had reacted. This included having cursed herself on many occasions; having accepted extremely low self-worth; and holding bitter resentments against members of her family.

It has been great to see Suzanne continue to move on through the Steps and to build a new history based upon the healing that has taken place. She continues to practise Step 10 and it has been a joy to see her change in the way she sees herself, how she is in her family, the work she does, and the way she is able to help and minister to others. Above all, she is now willing to admit, promptly, when she is in the wrong. In her new-found self-worth under God she is a changed person.

A prayer:

Dear Lord God, help me to do spot checks on my life daily and periodically. Help me always to remember you are changing me and are transforming me into your likeness with ever-increasing glory. Thank you that this comes from you, Lord God, from your Spirit. May I continue to be open to the change you want to bring in me. For Jesus Christ's sake. Amen.

Taking the 10th Step

Step 10. We continue to make personal inventories and when we are wrong promptly admit it.

This Step is our commitment to live by biblical principles. We decide to do so on a daily basis. We shall try to spot where we are about to go wrong. We shall admit where we have gone wrong. We will ask God to change us so that we go wrong less and less.

1. In daily situations, practise the following:
   (a) *Stop* (you know where you go wrong). You learn to spot which points in your life are likely to trigger you to sin. Learn to be proactive at this point rather than reactive. Remember how you have repented of actions such as these in the past.
   (b) *Think* (you know who can help). Recall how God has forgiven you for your past sins and has promised to remove your defects and shortcomings. Remember some of the promises of God, especially about how he will give you a way of escape (1 Corinthians 10:13).
   (c) *Pray* (you know the way forward). Now pray to God, asking for all you need to meet this situation and come through it successfully.

2. Take time each day to review your life before God. Do a mini-inventory each day, repenting of where you went wrong and sinned. The Alcoholics Anonymous *Big Book*[1] lists the following character defects for people to consider each day: selfishness; dishonesty; resentment; fear; jealousy; self-pity; greed; envy; depression; hatred; self-will; self-reliance. Acknowledge where you have been hurt and spot how you felt and how you reacted. Repent and forgive as necessary.

3. Make points 1 and 2 above part of your daily routine.

We seek through prayer and meditation to improve our conscious contact with God, praying only for knowledge of his will for us and the power to carry that out

"Come, all you who are thirsty, come to the waters; and you who have no money, come, buy and eat! Come, buy wine and milk without money and without cost. Why spend money on what is not bread, and your labour on what does not satisfy? Listen, listen to me, and eat what is good, and your soul will delight in the richest of fare. Give ear and come to me; hear me, that your soul may live. I will make an everlasting covenant with you, my faithful love promised to David. See, I have made him a witness to the peoples, a leader and commander of the peoples. Surely you will summon nations you know not, and nations that do not know you will hasten to you, because of the Lord your God, the Holy One of Israel, for he has endowed you with splendour."

Seek the Lord while he may be found; call on him while he is near. Let the wicked forsake his way and the evil man his thoughts. Let him turn to the Lord, and he will have mercy on him, and to our God, for he will freely pardon.

"For my thoughts are not your thoughts, neither are your ways my ways," declares the Lord. "As the heavens are higher than the earth, so are my ways higher than your ways and my thoughts than your thoughts. As the rain and the snow come down from heaven, and do not return to it without watering the earth and making it bud and flourish, so that it yields seed for the sower and bread for the eater, so is my word that goes out from my mouth: It will not return to me empty, but will accomplish what I desire and achieve the purpose for which I sent it. You will go out in joy and be led forth in peace; the mountains and the hills will burst into song before you, and all the trees of the field will clap their hands. Instead of the thornbush will grow the pine tree, and instead of briers the myrtle will grow. This will be for the Lord's renown, for an everlasting sign, which will not be destroyed."

Isaiah 55:1–13

Step 11 includes the whole Bible

This Step encourages us to improve our "conscious contact with God". It then seeks God's guidance, which is a natural progression from that close contact.

Step 11 is so important it can be said to embrace the whole teaching of the Bible. By taking Step 11 we are committing ourselves not just to seeking God for his healing and sorting, but also for his guidance and direction for the rest of our lives. This is essential as we continue to break out of our selfishness and start leading a selfless life.

If our attitude is one of "What can I get out of this?" we will not progress far with God. We have received much from him. We have experienced Jesus as our Saviour from the consequences of our sin, both in this life and for the next. He has come to heal, restore and change us. But now we must take matters further. We must ask God to be our Lord. Of course, we have already done this when we took Step 3 and in the intervening Steps we have decided to go his way. Here, however, we are specifically saying that if he is to be our Lord for the remainder of our life, then we must keep in contact with him on a day-to-day basis. We are to find out what he wants for our life so that we can be his servants and be under his rule.

For some people this is not an attractive prospect at all. Now that some of our pain has gone, we would like to take back control of our lives and do things our way. Sadly, some people come to know Jesus as their Saviour with all the blessings that this entails, only to drift away to do their own thing in subsequent years. Sometimes they turn full circle and return like the Prodigal Son, realizing that they cannot live successfully without God's Lordship. But God does not want us to go off. He wants us to hand over all of our life and will to him all the time.

The ear before the mouth

God says to us, "Listen, listen to me... Give ear and come to me; hear me, that your soul may live" (Isaiah 55:2–3).

In our relationship with God we do well to listen first and speak later. Some have said that is why God created us with two ears and yet only one mouth! Indeed, a baby learns to speak only through hearing first. The words the baby has heard most will then become the first words he or she speaks. When babies are born deaf they have great difficulty learning to speak.

Any relationship of any depth will be two-way. We must be careful not to see prayer as solely or primarily us speaking to God. In the Bible we will see many relationships between humans and God, and we will read of God speaking to them about his will and about his purpose for their lives and for the situations around them. Isaiah describes it like this: "He wakens me morning by morning, wakens my ear to listen like one being taught. The Sovereign Lord has opened my ears" (Isaiah 50:4–5).

It is no easy thing to hear from God and be taught by him. I believe the phrase "wakens my ear to listen" alludes to specific training for our ear so that we can pick up what God is saying to us today. If Isaiah needed his ear to be trained in order to hear God, how much more do we today, with all the hustle and bustle and noise of twenty-first century living. God's "still, small voice" can be drowned out very easily. Some people feel uncomfortable if there is no noise present. I often visit homes where the TV is rarely switched off. Even on a pre-funeral visit I may have to request that the TV sound be turned down. Our children listen to music hour on hour through personal CD players. It seems strange to them not to have some background music in their room.

The practice of having a "quiet time" with God each morning has been lost now for many people. Yet to have some time when we can solely concentrate on God and his word and contemplate and meditate for a period is invaluable to prepare us to enter the frantic world which itself has little time for God.

The example of biblical pray-ers

The Bible clearly shows us that those who were the mightiest in prayer also knew God well and had a period of training, particularly in listening. Jeremiah 15:1 singles out Moses and Samuel as effective intercessors. In the New Testament, when James looks for an example of a persistent pray-er, he speaks of Elijah (James 5:17). Moses was, under God, the maker and moulder of a nation and stood before him to plead for the people of Israel (Exodus 32:11-14). Samuel was the patient prophet who prepared the people for the first king of Israel. Elijah went out on a limb and opposed the king of Israel, King Ahab, in an attempt to stop the rot of idolatry. They were all effective pray-ers.

If we look first at Moses, we see that he was attuned to what God was saying and he had a long period of training in solitude. It could be argued that he had 40 years of solitude with just sheep, sands and stars as he worked as a shepherd for his father-in-law. Egypt's busy life was a thing of the past for him, and, surrounded by God's creation, he met with his God and heard his voice in the desert.

I once heard someone ask, "Are you strong enough to endure silence?" As someone brought up in a city and having lived in cities ever since, it is a rare treat to have real silence. I recall occasions when I have managed to get away to the Yorkshire Dales and been aware of God speaking to me through his word, through what I have seen and through what he has brought to my mind. The nearest I get to this on a daily basis is to get up early and, before life starts happening around me, I come before my God to hear from him.

Moses had 40 years of preparation, but also two specific periods of 40 days when he went up into the very presence of God on Mount Sinai. He was already in the place to hear what God wanted and subsequently came down to lead the people of Israel.

As for Samuel, he had an early training course in listening (1 Samuel 3). While still very young he became accustomed to hearing the voice of God. He was trained to distinguish between the voice of God and that of humans. Although Eli might not have done too well in bringing up his own sons, he displays God's wisdom in training Samuel to hear from God. This reminds us not only to think about our own ability to hear from God but also to seek to help our children from an early age. If we spend time around children we are aware that with a little direction they can hear from God and believe readily. I have now ceased to be surprised at some of the prayers our children wish to pray, in complete faith.

As far as the biblical record is concerned, Elijah seems to come from nowhere, yet it is the word of God that rules his life. "The word of the Lord came to Elijah: 'Go and present yourself to Ahab, and I will send rain on the land'" (1 Kings 18:1). All that transpired in the tremendous story of the showdown on Mount Carmel stems from God speaking to Elijah. Finally, Elijah says to the king, "Go eat and drink, for there is the sound of a heavy rain" (1 Kings 18:41). He is hearing what God has told him. Then, he prays persistently while going to look for the answer seven times. His ear heard, he was not afraid to speak out what he knew God was going to do, and his eye was expectant – but he kept on praying.

From the eye to the ear

For us, the eye and the ear often go together. What God has spoken to others in the past has now been written down for us in the Bible. There is a sense in which we "hear with our eyes", as God is still speaking to us through his word, the Bible. Yet we are not just to read the words but also to listen to the voice of God, "hearing" both what took place at the time of the writing and also how that word from God now relates to our life and situation. God will continue to reveal himself through the pages. The Bible therefore helps us not only to get to know about God, but also to get to know him personally.

God wants to communicate himself to us. Although there is often great benefit from going to Bible colleges or theological colleges, we must always be aware that the Bible is not a book primarily for analysis and critique. Some scholars have lost sight of this basic form of communication from God to us, through persistent sceptical analysis of the text.

The word of God is described as "the sword of the Spirit" (Ephesians 6:17). It is "living and active. Sharper than any double-edged sword, it penetrates even to dividing soul and spirit, joints and marrow; it judges the thoughts and attitudes of the heart" (Hebrews 4:12). As we read the Bible, God can speak right into our thoughts and our attitudes. God can touch our heart with his word.

There is an interesting phrase in 2 Samuel 23:10 when one of David's mighty men is being described. Eleazar is said to have "stood his ground... till his hand... froze to the sword". His hand and sword became one. What a picture of the man of God being as one with the sword of the Spirit, the word of God!

A Godly routine

It is no good waiting to feel like spending time in God's presence. Our feelings are so fickle that we could wait for ever! Instead, it is necessary to work out a routine that we will seek to keep to.

Firstly, we must decide which is the *best time* for us to spend some time alone with God. When can we be quiet with him? From experience, I have found this invariably will be first thing in a morning. Some say they find it impossible to get up early enough, and it can certainly be difficult to do this if you are on shift work. However, it is invaluable to spend some time with God before we get into the events and pressures of the day.

We must also be realistic as to how much time we can spend, and be aware that there will always be pressure for that period of time to be curtailed by the "urgent" (though not necessarily the "important"). If we have never really had a routine, then it is much better to build up from a short period of time in a morning to something longer in due course, rather than find you keep failing to make the time and ultimately get out of the habit. Start with ten minutes, then move towards 30 minutes after six months or so, then move to 60 minutes after a couple of years.

Secondly, spend time *looking at the Bible* itself rather than reading books about the Bible. Notes that help us read the Bible may well be useful, but let us start with the words of the Bible first and see what *we* believe God is saying to us through them before we refer to some other person's thoughts and insights.

Thirdly, if the eye and ear go together, then we need to *read prayerfully*. God may want to make some particular passage or verse stand out for us that particular day. It is amazing how God can use even familiar verses to speak some new truth to us. Many of us have heard someone else speak from a passage in the Bible and have been amazed not only by the message from God in those verses, but also as to why we had not spotted it earlier.

Step 11 talks about prayer, but also *meditation*. Meditation is not much talked about, yet it is a biblical concept referred to many times in the psalms (e.g. Psalm 119:15, 23, 27, 48, 78, 97, 99 and 148).

The word meditate really means "to mutter". Here we get the picture of someone speaking over and over again his thoughts of what he has seen and heard. The word meditate also has a sense of "to ruminate". This is what cows do when they "chew the cud". They bring up again some food they have previously digested and spend time chewing it over.

If we are going to meditate, and especially on God's word, then we can do this in a variety of ways. We can take a bird's eye view, an overview, of a whole book of the Bible and think our way through not only the context but also the truths that come from God, and then gradually apply them to our lives. This takes time. We should carve out ample time to let our thoughts flow and develop.

Meditation may also be on specific detail. We can go out into God's creation and meditate on him through that (e.g. Isaac in Genesis 24:63). Then, we can meditate on aspects of God and what he has done. There is God's unfailing love (Psalm 48:9), God's wonders (Psalm 119:27), God's laws (Psalm 119:48), God's promises (Psalm 119:148), and God's wonderful works (Psalm 145:5).

If we were to read an account of a particular event in Jesus' life on earth, we can even use our imagination to put ourselves into that scene. In John 21, we read of the disciples out fishing and then seeing Jesus on the shore. We can place ourselves in the boat with the other disciples. We can meditate a little on Peter and also on John, and get into some of the feelings that they would have experienced, especially after the events of the previous week. They had witnessed the crucifixion, the resurrection and the appearance of Jesus amongst them in the locked room. If we meditate on Peter, God may even speak to us about what it feels like to let Jesus down in our relationship with him, and yet to know his love and his desire to reinstate us to be that close friend and disciple again.

We can meditate on particular verses. An example is Psalm 3:5, where David says, "I lie down and sleep; I wake again, because the Lord sustains me." There seems little to meditate on here, until we realize that the heading for the psalm is "a psalm of David, when he fled from his son Absalom". How could David have slept in the midst of all that trauma (2 Samuel 15)? If such had happened to me I expect I would be tossing and turning, mad with worry. Yet by spending a little time in the company of David and his God, we start seeing what it means for us to be at peace in the midst of our sometimes troubled lives.

Likewise, how could Paul have written the letter to the Philippians with so much joy jumping from the pages (see Philippians 1:14, 1:25, 1:26, 2:2, 2:29, 4:1)? At the time of writing he was in prison, and yet the theme of the book is joy, or "rejoicing in the Lord". The word joy in its various forms occurs 16 times. As we ruminate on the letter to the Philippians, God will perhaps give us a different perspective on our own lives.

Finally, as we think of "improving our conscious contact with God", we should do so with an attitude of *obedience*. Jesus says to us in John 7:17, "If anyone chooses to do God's will, he will find out whether my teaching comes from God or whether I speak on my own." Jesus is saying that obedience is the key to hearing God's word. Having taken the previous Steps, here in Step 11 we are deciding to walk with God and to develop our relationship with him. It is a step of obedience.

Knowing God's will
It follows that if we deepen our relationship with God we will know his will for our lives. Nicky Gumbel, in the Alpha course and in his book *Questions of Life*[1], gives five helpful headings for making decisions. The first is *Commanding Scripture*. He starts with the Bible and emphasizes that we should submit to its teaching. He shows us not only that it is God's general revelation to us, but also that it can be used by God to speak to us specifically day by day. This is why the Bible is central to our daily routine.

Although our guidance may well come primarily from

God's word, Nicky Gumbel's four other headings are relevant for us. The second is *Compelling Spirit*. The Holy Spirit lives inside us when we become Christians. Consequently, he will be there to help us to see God's way.

As we spend time in prayer, he will impress upon our minds the importance of certain things. For instance, guidance can be subtle. It is the little nudge, "Why don't you call Richard?" However, when I do call Richard I don't say, "God told me to call you and this is what he told me to tell you." Instead, I just ask how he is doing. If he says, "I'm really doing well, but it's a bit inconvenient to talk at the moment so I'll get back to you later", I may then conclude, "It was indigestion, not God!" But on the other hand, it could be that he says, "It's great that you have called just now because I really need someone to talk to because..." and I think, "Well, that was from God." We then start building up experience that makes it easier for us to detect little nudges of the Spirit.

Thirdly, there is *Common sense*. We have been born with a brain and we do have to use our minds. God is in the business of renewing our minds (Romans 12:2). As we get to know more of what God is like, this knowledge informs our common sense. We can start to know what is good in his eyes.

The fourth point is the *Counsel of the saints*. Proverbs 12:15 says it is good to seek advice. Older and wiser Christians, especially those who may not necessarily see things as we do, may have a different but helpful perspective for us. Many people came to Jesus for advice, and sometimes he told them things they did not like. Jesus said to the rich young man in Mark 10:21, "Go, sell everything you have and give to the poor, and you will have treasure in heaven. Then come, follow me." We have to be prepared for others to challenge, not just confirm, our ideas.

Finally, there are *Circumstantial signs*. It says in Proverbs 3:5–6, "Trust in the Lord with all your heart and lean not on your own understanding; in all your ways acknowledge him, and he will make your paths straight." It is not always easy to see from our circumstances the way God wants us to go. In my experience there have been times when, looking back, circumstances have obviously been the way of God, yet there were all manner of difficulties along the way. For example, our church believed that we should buy some property for a drop-in youth centre. In the early stages this project met with both financial and planning-permission difficulties. Yet, as a church leadership, we continued to pray about the project and all its details and were quite open to the possibility that God might say that this was not the right place or project. Using the other four headings above, we continued to be convinced we were on the right track. In time, the money was provided and the permission was given.

Some people lay out "fleeces" as a method of guidance, following Gideon's example in Judges 6. I advise against it. The main reason is that when Gideon asked for a miracle, he asked in doubt and fear. He was not really sure he could trust God. That is not the point we should be coming from. God in his mercy did answer Gideon, but we cannot presume upon God's mercy. We know we can trust him.

Then there are feelings!

When we pray for God's will in our lives, our feelings are inevitably going to play a part. We are emotional people. However, our feelings are notoriously unreliable.

Recently I had to fly to the Isle of Man from Manchester. It's not very far and only takes about 35 minutes. It was raining all the way to Manchester and I was feeling fairly miserable. After waiting in the departure lounge for a while, I was feeling even more miserable. About ten minutes after we took off, we suddenly broke through the clouds and it was an amazing, lovely day up there. My spirits rose! Unfortunately, I was only above the clouds for ten minutes before we descended to the Isle of Man. It was raining again and my feelings plummeted. It reminded me of how fickle we are. My moods changed like a seesaw. It was much easier to believe in a wonderful, almighty creator God when I was up above the clouds than in the dreary departure lounge of Manchester airport. Yet God did not change for that ten minutes.

It takes persistence

Our persistence in prayers and in carrying out God's will should not be linked with what we are feeling. Recently God gave the steering group of ministers who pray for Bradford a number of objectives for seeing God's kingdom come in our city. However, the next time we met we found ourselves again seeking God's guidance in a way that seemed to deny that he had already spoken to us. Then one minister spoke up to say how fickle we were. We had to work towards the objectives previously revealed to us, and that required persistence. If God has spoken to us, then we need to see the matter through. It must break God's heart to see us flitting from one matter to another before anything has been fully accomplished.

As we saw with Elijah, he did not just pray and then go and look. He continued on his knees praying until the cloud was spotted and the rain was imminent (1 Kings 18:41–46).

God's will for us and the power to carry that out

In the Lord's Prayer we read, "Your will be done on earth as it is in heaven." In Step 11 we are asking for God's will to be done on our little piece of earth as well – where we are; in what we are going to be doing. We will only be in the right place for that to happen if we develop our relationship with God, namely improve our conscious contact with God.

In the Lord's Prayer we state our intention, "Your will be done", but also go on to seek his provision, "Give us today our daily bread", and ultimately acknowledge that it is his power that will make the difference. "For the kingdom, the power and the glory are yours now and for ever." Let us then pray the Lord's Prayer.

Our Father in heaven. Hallowed be your name. Your kingdom come. Your will be done on earth as it is in heaven. Give us today our daily bread. Forgive us our sins as we forgive those who sin against us. Lead us not into temptation but deliver us from evil. For the kingdom, the power and the glory are yours now and for ever. Amen.

Taking the 11th Step

Step 11. We seek through prayer and meditation to improve our conscious contact with God, praying only for knowledge of his will for us and the power to carry that out.

Step 11 encourages us to get to know God better. We make a decision to develop our relationship with him in our daily lives.

1. How good are you at hearing God? Do you find silence easy? Start to develop times of silence between you and God.

2. What is your daily routine with God? What length of time can you commit yourself to? What difference do you hope to see in your routine in a year's time?

3. Decide to try meditation if you have never done it. How are you going to start? An overview of a book of the Bible? A story from Jesus' life? A particular verse?

4. Offer yourself as a living sacrifice to God (Romans 12:1) so that he can show you his "good, pleasing and perfect will" (Romans 12:2). Now try and memorize the following principles of guidance
   – Commanding Scripture
   – Compelling Spirit
   – Common sense
   – Counsel of the saints
   – Circumstantial signs

5. Honestly think through before God how much you are ruled by your feelings and how easily you can be distracted from spending time in contact with God. Repent of these.

6. Pray through the Lord's Prayer phrase by phrase and think how each applies to your life.

Step **12**

Having had a spiritual awakening as a result of these Steps, we try to carry this message to others and to practise these principles in all our affairs

So from now on we regard no-one from a worldly point of view. Though we once regarded Christ in this way, we do so no longer. Therefore, if anyone is in Christ, he is a new creation; the old has gone, the new has come! All this is from God, who reconciled us to himself through Christ and gave us the ministry of reconciliation: that God was reconciling the world to himself in Christ, not counting men's sins against them. And he has committed to us the message of reconciliation. We are therefore Christ's ambassadors, as though God were making his appeal through us. We implore you on Christ's behalf: Be reconciled to God. God made him who had no sin to be sin for us, so that in him we might become the righteousness of God.

2 Corinthians 5:16–21

There is a great similarity between this passage from 2 Corinthians 5 and the wording of Step 12. It reminds us that we have become a new creation and because of that we are now reconcilers, God's ambassadors here on earth. We are to carry this message of reconciliation to others in the world.

A spiritual awakening for all

Some of us may have had a spiritual awakening before we looked at these Steps. Others may have gone through the Steps and met with God during the process. We have become aware that life is not just physical, it is spiritual. We have come into contact with the creator God and moved from knowing about him to actually knowing him personally. We have started experiencing him in our lives and become aware of how he can change us, and of the plans he has for us.

Particularly, we have come to see that Jesus is the revelation of God to us. By looking to him as he is revealed in the Gospels, we have acknowledged him as our Saviour and our Lord. We have therefore come to God, who loves us deeply, and surrendered our wills and our lives to him so that he can cleanse us, change us and lead us on.

Step 12 takes into account all that has gone before and leaves us with the intention and commitment to tell others about the good news of the freedom we have found in God. Step 12 follows the pattern of the Gospels in that at the end there is the "great commission" to go out and tell others. (See Matthew 28:18–20; Mark 16:15–18; Luke 24:46–49; John 20:21–23.)

Our vision statement at St John's encapsulated this 12th Step, and also mirrors 2 Corinthians 5. The statement is "To know God, to show God, to share God."

To know God

"Therefore if anyone is in Christ, he is a new creation; the old has gone, the new has come!" (2 Corinthians 5:17). God is there to be known.

Perhaps there was a particular time when suddenly it all fell into place and we realized that God loved us and Jesus had died for our sins on the cross. Maybe we have come to know God by a growing awareness of how much we are loved. Whatever our experience, we know he has come into our lives and sent his Holy Spirit to fill us. We know that we are not alone, as he is with us all the time.

There are as many different conversion experiences as there are Christians. Sometimes the awareness of God's presence and love can be accompanied by a physical experience. I have known people break out into a sweat, or start crying, or burst into tears, or fall onto the floor, or be unable to control their body shaking.

But others have looked as though they have experienced nothing. I remember one woman who had her eyes shut and looked bored or asleep. Yet later she revealed it was as if she had been transported into the very throne room of God and was staring into the Father's eyes! People have had amazing experiences of God while not showing anything physically. The physical reactions and the feelings do not matter. What is important is that we *know* we have had a spiritual awakening and have started to know again this God in whose image we have been created.

As some people have gone through these Steps they have had dramatic spiritual awakenings. Some have known their guilt lifting off them as their sins are forgiven. They have found shame disappearing. Others have known a dramatic cleansing and healing, after their hurt and damage has been brought before the Lord. For some this spiritual awakening has been part of conversion itself, whereas for others who already had a relationship with God it has been a subsequent spiritual awakening. They had never experienced the release because they had never looked at their lives in such detail before.

Some people find God speaking to them about their worth in him. I can think of an elderly lady who had spent her life trying to achieve things and be good enough. It was a release for her to know that she was already accepted and loved by God. This was a spiritual awakening for her and has changed the whole of her demeanour. Instead of being someone who was striving for acceptance not only with God but also with others, she is now happy in herself. Her contentment is now a springboard for serving the Lord. The old has gone and the new come.

For others, though, the spiritual awakening has hardly been perceptible. But now at Step 12 they can look back and see that yes, they have changed and have come to know God. They do know his forgiveness, cleansing and healing. But when did they actually become a true follower of Jesus? That does not matter.

When my wife and I moved to a town in the south of England and decided to join a church we spent some time with the vicar. He wanted to know the date and time of our respective conversions. This proved difficult for my wife, as she did not have a specific conversion experience. She had grown up in a Christian home and had always known God with her and had always accepted Jesus as her Saviour and her Lord. Yes, there were times when she had decided to keep on walking with God rather than to go a different path, but could they be called a conversion experience? The vicar had rather a narrow view of this and I think was not sure whether she was truly converted and a born-again Christian! Looking back, we may not know the time of our spiritual awakening but we all *know* there has been one. That is what is important.

However, a few people over the years have said to me that they have done all the Steps but not had any spiritual awakening. The common factor has always been that in truth they have not really completed Step 4, Step 4½ and Step 5. I recall one man who had done a very thorough Step 4 and had written everything down. Nevertheless, he had never quite got round to meeting up with someone to confess what he had written down. He had not done Step 5. Another had made a good stab at completing Step 4 but could not bring himself to write down the one sin that he was really ashamed of. There was no way he wanted to share that with anyone else.

I recall a woman who just could not face looking at her relationship with her father. She was scared of the pain she knew lay in that relationship. She had tried to continue through the Steps without dealing with this fundamental area of damage in her life.

Praise God that all these people subsequently received power from God and an awareness of his love for them to the extent that they could move on. Their testimony is that they had a spiritual experience, an awakening, at a later time.

Finally, God does not want us to stay still and rely on past spiritual experience. This is just the beginning and that is why it is called an "awakening" in Step 12. We have woken up spiritually and God now wants to develop our spiritual lives and to make us useful for him.

To show God

"God made him who had no sin to be sin for us, so that in him we might become the righteousness of God" (2 Corinthians 5:21). Step 12 speaks of the necessity "to practise these principles in all our affairs". When we are converted, or when we have a spiritual awakening, that is not the end of the matter. At conversion we begin our eternal life. We begin the path of holiness, and the process of sanctification. Peter reminds us that we are to be holy: "But just as he who called you is holy, so be holy in all you do; for it is written: 'Be holy because I am holy'" (1 Peter 1:15–16).

Before we rush off to tell other people about our experience and about the good news that is not just for us but for them too, we need to make sure that we are practising the principles we have learnt. In other words, are we showing God in our lives?

In Matthew 28, when Jesus gave the great commission, he said that the disciples were to teach others to obey that which he had commanded them. So they had to pass on what they had learnt from Jesus in the time they had been with him. That included his holiness and his principles of living.

Books about evangelism often speak of the stages that are involved. One example is "presence, proclamation, persuasion". In carrying the message to others we do need to be aware that presence is the vital first ingredient. Yet what does our presence actually portray? We are to show the holiness of God in our lives, and that the old has gone and the new has come.

Those who know us well will be looking to see how we have changed. They will want to know whether this new creation is lasting or just a flash in the pan. We have to earn the right to do any proclamation by first of all being *present* with them. This may be just a matter of fact in that we work alongside them or live next door. But it is also more than that. It is helping and supporting when they have needs. It is listening to them and being interested. All this involves spending time with them.

Statistics show that it is very rare for someone to be converted without having been close to Christians for a period of time before any proclamation takes place. People are looking to see what we do. They are listening to our words. They are seeing whether our words and our actions match up.

Jesus says, "A new command I give you: Love one another. As I have loved you, so you must love one another. All men will know that you are my disciples if you love one another" (John 13:34–35). As we do this and move from a selfish, self-centred life to one that cares for those around us and shares the love that God is giving to us, then those around us will start to take notice.

As we "practise these principles in all our affairs" we should use particular Steps to meet particular situations. Think of the Steps as a bag of golf clubs. An experienced golfer can know which club to take out of the bag for a particular shot. His eyes get used to how far he can hit a ball with a particular iron or a particular wood. If he hits it right, it *should* go straight towards the flag.

The 12 Steps are a bit like that. At each point in our lives, we say, "Which one do I need in this situation?" When life seems to be taking over and we are becoming stressed out – my life is unmanageable (Step 1). I suddenly realize I have been trying to get my own way and have got considerably frustrated – I need to hand over my will and life to God again (Step 3). I become aware of having hurt someone and our relationship is not the same as it used to be – I need to make amends (Steps 8 and 9). That habit is creeping back into my life and it's not good – I need to humbly ask God to remove all my shortcomings (Steps 6 and 7). Once again, I have a particular sin that seems to have a grip on me. It's my little secret – I need to admit it and confess it (Step 4 and Step 5).

Going through the Steps hopefully will be a life-changing experience. However, they are still there for us to use in our continued quest for holiness. They are tools (or clubs) to continue to move us on.

To share God

"And he has committed to us the message of reconciliation. We are therefore Christ's ambassadors, as though God were making his appeal through us" (2 Corinthians 5:19–20). How do we take this message to others? We don't always have to do it by going onto the streets and telling people! We don't necessarily need to go door to door! The main way will be talking naturally with people we know. We have a network of people that we are in contact with each week, including family, friends, workmates and neighbours. Then we can help people, too, or listen to them. We can get involved in projects that help people in need. We can make a specific effort to be where people are – at the night school, at the bowling club, at aerobics, at the slimmers' meeting. We are to show God's love in our lives and speak when necessary of how we have come to experience that.

A vital part of the recovery process through Alcoholics Anonymous is attending the meetings. Here, members of AA will share their experiences of what they were like, what is happening to them now and how the Steps are important to them. In the Christian church we have seen the value of testimony. When we have guest services we often ask someone to give a short account of what God has been doing in their lives. This is proclamation.

We have probably heard dramatic testimonies of the change that God has brought about in a person's life. Unfortunately, sometimes the person's life before they met with God comes across as rather more exciting than what they experienced after meeting with God! The testimony has centred on the titillating, the shocking or the dramatic.

But effective testimony centres on God and what he has done for us. This can be dramatic, but not necessarily so. Over the years at St John's, Bowling, I have tried to convince members of the congregation that they have a dynamic testimony in the "ordinariness" of their lives. It is dynamic because that is the sort of life that most people lead. Most lives are fairly ordinary and to see God break in and change them from being a "nice, boring person" to a lovely, purposeful person is in itself a testimony of great value.

The testimony also needs to be short. We need to train ourselves to be able to tell of what God has done in our lives in two minutes! We need to be able to give our testimony at a bus stop and finish it before the bus comes (that's if it's on time!).

We also need to talk of what God is doing in our lives today, not just what he has done in the past. Some people's testimony relates only to what God did several years ago. Perhaps we should be banned from talking about past experiences, and confine ourselves instead to what God has been doing in the last month. People may be struck by a dramatic change but they are even more struck by our experience of God today.

Our sharing is both presence and proclamation, but it is rarely our job to persuade people to become Jesus' disciples. Maybe they are persuaded by the pain and desperation in their lives. Or it may be that God by his Holy Spirit is convicting them of sin, righteousness and judgement.

Someone once said, "You can keep God only by giving him away." Over the years we have tried to build into our values at St John's the importance of sharing the good news of the Gospel with others. Not only is this of obvious benefit to those around us but it also benefits us. It helps us to continue to change from being selfish to selfless. It puts our problems, pressures and pleasures in perspective. If we do not pass on this good news about God, then our Christian life can become stagnant, lifeless and horrible. No wonder Jesus talked about living water coming *from* us. He told his disciples to "go". God is asking us to do the same.

Be very careful then how you live

Finally, let us sum up Step 12 in Paul's words. "Be very careful, then, how you live – Not as unwise but as wise, making the most of every opportunity, because the days are evil. Therefore do not be foolish, but understand what the Lord's will is. Do not get drunk on wine, which leads to debauchery. Instead, be filled with the Spirit. Speak to one another with psalms, hymns and spiritual songs. Sing and make music in your heart to the Lord, always giving thanks to God the Father for everything, in the name of our Lord Jesus Christ. Submit to one another out of reverence for Christ" (Ephesians 5:15–21).

The days are evil and we can so easily fall. We therefore need to be careful how we live. These Steps enable us to seek help. They are not just for people who have over-whelming problems in their lives. They are for all who call themselves Christians. The truth is that we are powerless against sin and that without God our lives will be unmanageable. From this starting point – at Step 1 – we can follow the programme of 12^{1}/$_{2}$ Steps: Steps that are based on biblical truth and will bring us recovery.

As we do, we will find God meeting with us and coming more and more into our lives. So let us end by calling upon him, asking that we be filled once more with his Spirit. Then we can start submitting to each other out of reverence for Christ. Knowing God and being filled with his Spirit will enable us to show God in our lives, and then to share him with others. It is a hurting world out there, and it needs God's ambassadors.

A prayer:

Dear Lord Jesus, I thank you and praise you because I have met with you. Lord, I'm sure I need to meet with you in a deeper way still and to hold nothing back. Lord, come in and lead me by your Spirit. Thank you that you love me, that you want the best for me, you want freedom and release for me and you want to use me powerfully in this evil and dark world. May I shine like the stars in the universe for you. I ask this in Jesus' name. Amen.

Taking the 12th Step

Step 12. Having had a spiritual awakening as a result of these Steps, we try to carry this message to others and to practise these principles in all our affairs.

Here we acknowledge that it is good to have a relationship with God, and we commit ourselves to deepening that relationship and letting God change us so we reach our full potential. We shall also carry this good news to those around us.

1. Spend a little time before God looking back over your life and seeing where and when you first got to know him, and what have been the significant milestones in your walk with him since.

2. Thank God for your history of coming to *know God*. Humbly ask God for his continued revelation to you about himself and his plans for your life.

3. Look back and ask God to show you how you have changed and become more like him. Take hold of the encouragement that comes from particular victories over habitual sin and changes of attitude over time. It's good to record these in your notebook so that in the "down" times you can return to them and be encouraged. Ask God to continue to change you. Commit yourself to using the $12^{1}/_{2}$ Steps as necessary to continue the change in you. Commit yourself to reading the Bible on a regular basis so that God can apply his principles of living into your life.

4. Ask God to give you a heart for those who are lost. Also spend a little time preparing your account of what God has done in your life and make sure the glory goes to him! Prepare a final list (!) of those people who are in your network – i.e. family, friends, neighbours, workmates, etc. Ask God to give you opportunities to tell them about what God has done.

5. Finally, thank God for what he has done in your life and again give your will and your life over to him. Commit yourself to be an ambassador for God in this dark, hurting world in which we live.

Notes

Introduction
1. *Body & Cell*, by Howard Astin, Monarch, 1998.

Chapter 1
1. *Pride and Perjury*, by Jonathan Aitken, HarperCollins, 2000, p. 69f.

Chapter 3
1. *Journey into Life*, by Norman Warren, Kingsway.
2. *A Hunger for Healing*, by Keith Miller, HarperSanFrancisco, 1991.

Chapter 4$^1/_2$
1. *Parenting with Intimacy*, by David and Teresa Ferguson, Paul and Vicky Warren, and Terri Ferguson, Victor Books, 1995.

Chapter 5
1. *Luther's Works*, (Muhlenberg Press, Philadelphia, 1959), Volume 36, p. 86.

Chapter 7
1. *Body & Cell*, by Howard Astin, Monarch, 1998.

Chapter 9
1. *Alcoholics Anonymous*, Alcoholics Anonymous World Services Inc., 3rd Edition, 1976, p. 82.

Chapter 10
1. *Alcoholics Anonymous*, Alcoholics Anonymous World Services Inc., 3rd Edition, 1976.

Chapter 11
1. *Questions of Life*, by Nicky Gumbel, Kingsway, 1993.